Dedicated to the
Future.
I hope you are
Blessed
with
Unity, Love, Peace, Harmony
&
Positive Vibrations.

TO BE OR NOT TO BE BLACK?

BY

JC KAMAU

CONTENTS

INTRODUCTION

In February 2020 I was reminded of the words of Malcolm X as it was the anniversary of his death on the 21st of that month. This prompted me to reacquaint myself with his speeches via YouTube. One of which is in this book as it and the others reminded me society hasn't progressed as far as people of African descent would like. Also, I watched the debate Mr X participated in at the Oxford Union. During it he dissected the famous William Shakespeare quote "To Be Or Not To Be That Is The Question". He explains that this question is whether not to go against or with the hierarchy? Whether or not to be a righteous thinking person who fights for freedom or not? This is the dilemma that Black people have to ask in a time when they feel oppressed. This led me to contemplate on the notions I've had on this society over the years. These clarifying thoughts were stored for a long time. Realizations I have had after meditating and I started to compile them together in my mind with the option to write them down at some point.

   Also, after my journey to Egypt, where I felt spiritually high, I came back to Britain and felt sorrow for the majority of my compatriots as I could now blatantly see spiritual ineptness emanating from most factions of society. These murmurings in my mind were allowed to spread to paper via pen due to the lockdown in 2020. As there was less to do work wise, I had the time to sit and write what I wanted. Without distractions or major interruptions. I started writing about this spiritual ineptitude that I witnessed and was going to write the second paper To Be Or Not To Be Black? about the problems I feel we face in this European controlled system we live in; they would have been two separate papers but George Floyd got murdered in horrendous circumstances. The fall out of which made me hasten my writing of Spiritually Inept

Society so I could get to writing my views about this hot topic. Then I also had another moment of clarity that showed me the two essays were connected. Black people will never be in a position we deserve to be in while this society is devoid of truly spiritual people who want to strive for Peace and Love and understand we all are equal in the eyes of The Most High. So, this persuaded me to put the two together.

When I read it back to myself, I thought it wouldn't be good to just let this be writing for fun. My feelings were this is necessary to be in the public domain to help fuel the conversations that will hopefully lead to positive changes for all people. Hence this became a book.

I myself have been predominantly writing poetry for the last few years. It does show within these prose. My overall goal with my poems is why I chose to share this book with you. I have acquired an acquaintance with The Most High. This leads me to think in a spiritual way which differs significantly from the material minded. So, I try to open up these material thinkers to a different, more uplifting way of expressing the self & experiencing the world we live in. Hoping to bring these people out of the doldrums so they are closer to being on a par with the higher minds that created spiritual classics that people like myself read, watch, listen too to be inspired by. So, I hope that after reading this it moves you forward to attain wisdom and overstanding. Even if you considered yourself a deep thinker before reading this or not. I want everyone to be able to be closer to the place where balance resides so that we human beings can be in tune with all the spiritual forces as well as the material. So, we all can appreciate each other the way we should. Looking at, seeing that everything natural on planet earth is a blessing from The Most High. Enjoy.

Part 1

Ignorance is Bliss?

The Black experience is not great, it can be quite upsetting for many at times, due to the disadvantages and obstacles put in place by a predominately racist elite. This construct is something only implemented when people of African descent intermingle with western society. When amongst themselves and only interacting with people of their own race, the colour of their skin isn't an issue. Even though there may be different shades they do not consider that to be of detriment to the character of the human being. It has no bearing to what type of individual they are in these countries where Africans supposedly control the governmental system. They have people that are highly educated as well as not. These are dark skinned people from all echelons of life. From the doctors to the dustbin cleaners. That's why Richard Pryor spoke about his epiphany during his journey to Africa.

"When I was in Africa, this voice came to me and said, Richard, what do you see? I said, I see all types of people. The voice said, But do you see any niggers? I said, No. It said, Do you know why? 'Cause there aren't any."

Richard Pryor

Also, we must consider that neither of the European words used to describe African people are from an African language. If you called an Amharic, Arabic, Swahili, Twee, Yoruba, Xhosa speaker Black they would look at you blankly due to the language barrier.

Now it's usually the people who have not that tend to want to leave this plentiful continent and seek pastures new in other more affluent countries. These individuals are able to grasp the Black experience. They start to feel what they have only really seen via the media. What African-Caribbean & African-American people have become accustomed to.

Since the advent of the international slave trade, Europeans have changed the way they treat people of African descent. During these horrific times, to justify it to the general public they had to start a disgusting propaganda campaign. Vilifying & ridiculing the African to the extent they are seen as lesser human beings in the eyes of others. With these tools they developed a separation between the races, the social inequality created makes it very difficult for people to interact properly with each other. Even though the work done helped in a major way to create wealth, the Europeans have still continued to widen the divide between the races.

If you check the Greeks, Persians, Kamau (Ancient Egyptian), Kushite's and the many other tribes of the ancient world, you see they all had respectful interactions that were not disrupted due to the colour of their skin tone. In fact, as well as conflicts that arose, there were many instances where they would have intermarriages between the kingdoms. Princesses marrying into another house to instigate a peace accord between the 2 cultures. If only things were that easy now.

Another example were also the Moors. Not only did they inspire Shakespeare to write Othello about one of their Kings, but they also helped to bring influential changes to European society before they were betrayed. Introducing/teaching them how to mass produce paper, creating & distributing books across Europe. Algebra & Alcohol are of Moorish descent & showed them how to build castles as well as many other valuable things people would be surprised to find out they were taught by the Black Moors. The rock of Gibraltar is named after a Black Moor. There were many instances in the days of yore that shows that these prejudices were man made and not instincts.

After slavery was abolished unfortunately the hierarchy chose to continue on with the unfair representation as well as not investing in the people that they had just finished using to administer high amounts of wealth. Instead, money was used to compensate the slave owners who then went on to use some of the tactics, founded in the slave fields, in factories which helped them kick start the Industrial Revolution in Europe. Also, they put the ex-slaves back to work. They, who didn't receive a penny for reparations, were just paid a small wage for the same crappy work. But to those poor people it was essential as they didn't get offered a trip home and they were stuck in those foreign lands needing to earn to eat. But the people they were asking had many years of propaganda contamination in their brains which stopped them from sharing in the spoils and giving them reparations and treating them in a humane way. This act infused the mentality of the racist as the Africans were economically low. Poverty kept them on a level far below the people who had used them to make the money to live with the ability to feel superior to others.

We mustn't forget the impact knowledge of gunpowder had. This was the other thing that gave them the superiority complex. Unlike they did in Asia, (Using it to beautify the sky with fireworks) they created evil weapons that curtail life such as the cannon & the gun. Leading them to eventually implement our current weapons of major destruction. This military might gave them control over other countries which has made the European mind very arrogant & rude. Add that to the survival of the fittest/separatist thought processes which makes them suspicious & prejudice even amongst their own. A concoction fuelled by the way they undermined the Africans with their false scripted words eventually developed into what we call racism.

The propaganda campaign was aimed mainly for the working class. To stop them insinuating they were being treated on a par with the African slave they tried to depict them as better, more appreciated than the slaves and subsequently leading them to have a disdain when slavery was abolished. Stemming from an unwarranted fear of their livelihoods being taken. This hostility has continued as we are still waiting for the hierarchy to administer the truth about history. When they fabricated African history, human history became falsified giving it a distorted view. This unfairness has left a vicious state of affairs, leading them to bask in a stupefied glory. Blindness which makes them feel their pale skin makes them superior.

We Blacks have lost a lot due to slavery. Our connection with Africa was whipped out of us. At the beginning of the passage, we were probably quite aggravated. We had just been kidnapped & thrown in a hole not knowing why or where the journey will end. There were many African mutinies on slave ships. So eventually the slavers would have been prepared for this anger. They had tactics to destabilise these acts of aggression. Chaining them together & making them watch while they beat, rape or murder a fellow slave. Knowing that if you either disrespect the overseer or become sick you could be thrown overboard would make many people hold in their rage. Which is why by the time they got to Barbados (The first island you come across when travelling from Ghana via boat so it became the place most slaves would pass through before being moved onto another island to become a slave) they were far more subdued. Eventually they would lose their African names being given a European first name & then the slave owners name as the surname. After that the connection with their descendants would diminish further. They would eventually lose their African name as that would have been forbidden to speak. Hundreds of years later those whose families would have been once African named have absolutely no idea what their names used to be or even worse, we have no idea to what part of Africa is our ancestral home. This has led to a deep separation between the people who were taken from Africa & the ones who weren't. A man from Atlanta could be in conversation with a woman from Timbuktu & not know they are somehow related.

People forget we were not allowed to learn other things about the place & culture we were in as the slave masters knew education would lead to a revolt. Which eventually happened. But the only thing we were allowed to see was the Bible. This was used to keep the slaves subjugated as they were given an abridged version with key parts taken out so it wouldn't inspire them to fight against the oppression. The passages they were afforded to see helped to keep them in line for a long period. The Bible was first used by King James to keep the British subjects in line. When they saw it worked, they thought it best to use it during slavery. Creating a slave mentality that kept these people subservient to them. But this could not last for all of the people as many still had the spirit they left Africa with. That power could not be beaten out of them & helped them to engage in destroying the slave trade.

In Europe they always show how liberal the Abolitionist where in the 1800's. But fail to mention the inspiring freedom fighters such as Toussaint Overture of Haiti & Nat Turner of North America. Whose uprisings against the slave owners, fighting against & killing the overseers made so much waves they couldn't continue the slave trade.

Because the French spent so much money and effort fighting the Haitians and they were not making any money from the slave trade, the Brits became quite wealthy and held the monopoly in the slave trade at that time of the Haitian revolution. But once the conflict with Haiti was over the French wanted to get back in the game. But to stop that & subsequently losing more wealth to the French again they, The British government chose to join the fight against slavery & helped the Abolition movement.

The problems for dark skinned people tend to arise when associating with the colder climates & its inhabitants. When venturing into these places they have to make changes to their outlook. Once you are faced with a race that 1, has a dislike of you even before you have anything to say and 2, they don't call themselves European. The term they manifested was White people. Which leads them to see others by the tone of their skin. Something we hadn't done before as they are all the same when amongst people in their homeland. In response to this new interaction, terms had to be invented to describe ourselves. All these names are mainly to communicate with Europeans. There have been many terms since the inaugural scientific description Negroid. Negro, Coloured and of course the bastardized nigger/nigga as well as others, but the one that the majority have found solace in is Black.

Coming to prominence in the American civil rights campaign. Stemming from the anger of oppression, The Black Power movement came from the mind state that was in direct opposition to the white supremacist regime that fuelled America & the European economic so-called democratic system. The clandestine way they controlled the masses made Marcus Mosiah Garvey, who is considered one of the first civil rights leaders in the 1920's, think it appropriate to speak to Imperial Kleagle Edward Young Clarke the then head of the Ku Klux Klan. Mr Garvey understood that he was a major leader in America and would be more influential in making changes to the judicial & economic system in America for Black people than any other white person. He knew that country and the majority of western governments leaders had racist standpoints. This is still prevalent in the leaders of European nations. Donald Trump, Boris Johnson have made abhorrent comments and even though she travelled to many African countries with him, the Queen's husband is a known racist.

This racism at the highest level can be combated with a strong anti-white supremacy movement that is as powerful as the propaganda campaign that started this problem in the 1400's. Many have tried but did not totally succeed in their endeavours.

Mutulu Shakur, Tupac's step father & some other unfortunate souls like Assata Shakur tried & failed with The Black Liberation army. Probably inspired by the Black Power movement whose leaders were Huey P Newton, Bobby Seale & Eldridge Cleaver (Who ran for President) & later Fred Hampton Jr. They were radical enough to stand up to a system they felt wanted them dead. As well as manifesting uplifting progressive projects for their communities, they & their counterparts were willing to defend their brothers & sisters from the harsh realities of racist America. They realised unity is strength. Seeing it work well during the civil rights struggle they added the aspect of defence through arming themselves with similar weaponry that the oppressors were using on them. This did help for a period of time. They did have real power that was being listened too.

The problem for them was not everyone maintained the fight. Firstly, disunity crept its ugly head into the party coupled with some who felt putting food on their family's tables more important. They found low paid work keeping them in the poverty trap. Others chose to assimilate into the system, becoming capitalist and acquiring the money to move out of poverty trap. What made the situation worse for many is they were bombarded with illegal highly addictive drugs. Another way to escape the poverty trap for a saddened mind. Which meant more people unable to be a part of the quest for racial equality.

Even with all the obstacles, The Black power movement transcended its beginnings in America and travelled the world. Especially as the media entities opened up a cultural dialogue making it even more necessary for people of the world to be named Black instead of utilising the actual place where their cultural heritage came from like the Chinese, Japanese & Indians. (Like Africans they have multiple shades of complexions. Some even darker than some so-called Black people) They used this term Black that describes all displaced people of Africa and still connects them with their home continent just like the opposition, the Europeans of America and their white counterparts across the globe. The thing was when taking on board this term they didn't understand the negative undertones that it would have. There was a lot of dark nuances associated with the colour Black. Especially when you look it up in the dictionary and see how much positive connotations there are when looking up the word white. This negative/positive conflict is in essence part of the problem between the races in modern times. Black and its people are seen in a negative light. An example of this is over 50 years ago Malcolm X speaking about how the media generally portrays the Negro as a criminal, alcoholic reprobate that society could do without.

"One of the shrewd ways that they use the press to project us in the eye or image of a criminal: they take statistics. And with the press they feed these statistics to the public, primarily the white public. Because there are some well-meaning persons in the white public as well as bad-meaning persons in the white public. And whatever the government is going to do, it always wants the public on its side, whether it's the local government, state government, federal government. So, they use the press to create images. And at the local level, they'll create an image by feeding statistics to the press -- through the press showing the high crime rate in the Negro community. As soon as this

high crime rate is emphasized through the press, then people begin to look upon the Negro community as a community of criminals.

And then any Negro in the community can be stopped in the street. "Put your hands up," and they pat you down. You might be a doctor, a lawyer, a preacher, or some other kind of Uncle Tom. But despite your professional standing, you'll find that you're the same victim as the man who's in the alley. Just because you're Black and you live in a Black community, which has been projected as a community of criminals. This is done. And once the public accepts this image also, it paves the way for a police-state type of activity in the Negro community. They can use any kind of brutal methods to suppress Blacks because "they're criminals anyway." And what has given this image? The press again, by letting the power structure or the racist element in the power structure use them in that way."

*"The **media's** the most powerful entity on earth. They have the power to make the innocent guilty and to make the guilty innocent." **Media** has been a tool that has proven to influence the minds, ideas, behaviours and attitudes of the masses."*

Malcolm X.

Those statements could be said now about the way the Media; Film & Television industries portray Black people. What makes it worse is these are all aspects of their economic system that arose regardless of race. Europeans are criminals also. The Italian mafia are still going to this day but do all Italians get tarnished with the same brush. It's not just the Europeans whose economic culture breeds criminality. Do all Japanese people get accused of being members of the Yakuza? Crime is a major part of our society. It goes hand in hand with poverty. Hence its association with crime. Black criminals do not get revered in the same way such as the Kray Twins. No Black criminal would get a funeral; members of the aristocracy would be proud of the way Reggie Kray did.

Personally, I don't think any of these criminals should be held in high esteem. What I do understand is amongst the poor these criminals come in handy. Especially for Black people who have been poor for generations ever since being brought into the western system. They were never welcomed with open arms by the people that made astronomical amounts of money from free labour. The wealthy, who they have been watching show off their material wealth, have been duping them into thinking the acquisition of material goods is needed. This craving for what European lifestyle feels like has left the poor people wanting these extortionately priced things that most cannot afford to pay for. So, they find illegal outlets to buy what they want. This leads to so-called criminal acts that get scrutinised by the media. When these types of people are exploited in the media without showing either well-adjusted upstanding members of society or outspoken freedom fighters, people who don't associate with these races on a regular basis get used to seeing those negative images and tend to brandish anyone that looks similar to these Black stereotypes as one. When this brush is wiped on all they see, it makes it hard for darker skinned people to move around in these European countries with freedom. There will always be the problem of suspicion. The white people will have an instant suspicion of a Black person which can breed situations that cause harm to the person of African descent or hinder the person from living freely. As well as that, Black people, no matter if they have been educated to a high standard or have become wealthy, unfairly have to go through life feeling, wondering if they will be suspected of being a stereotypical Black person when they are not. (Which is extremely stressful & depressing) Fearful of the reactions of white individuals who are ignorant enough to stop someone from feeling human, free. They are left with the question is this person going to accept me for who I am or disrespect me for the colour of me skin? (Anxiety that gets accentuated when the police drive or walk by) And in parts of the world like America or Brazil am I going to die because I'm Black?

A lot of Black people have an issue with what I call Africanaphobia. The fear of being 100% themselves all the time. We know our cultures are quite different to the European. When we are around other Black people, we feel free to be ourselves but once we are in the vicinity of white people some tend to hold back. Why don't we all feel comfortable enough to be ourselves around them? Over the years we have been told that we are not as good as them so we try to do the things they do & act like them especially when we are around them with the hope that this would be accepted. We have changed the way we do our hair, to be neater we cut, chemicalize it or place someone else's old hair on top of the head to feel some social acceptance. We don't realise that when you are not being yourself the person you are trying to impress wont respect you as much as if you are yourself wholeheartedly. We have to learn that there is absolutely nothing wrong with being Black. It is truly beautiful. Skin blessed by the sun whenever we want. Realise that African people are disunited broken. Once a highly educated Loved and Peaceful place. Now the great lands race is held up in suburbia with a repressed culture. From our fundamental fruits of knowledge, we've had an exclusion, which has led to a confusion manifested by the mass unmelanated mirage. We buy into this commercialized illusion that has left a large percentage of us bewildered.

At some point we must feel free to learn about our cultures and not feel we are going against the European field of thought. We must not care if a white person will like us if we are in love with aspects of our culture so much, we want to express it as much as possible. White people don't care when offending other cultures. They will happily shout about it. Prince Harry (Real name Henry) happily went to a party wearing a Nazi jacket. He was intelligent to know what people would think of him if they saw him in that fashion but he wasn't bothered by the thoughts of others at that time. That is in his heritage which I assume he was expressing at the time. Perhaps he was giving thanks to his grandmother's uncle who abdicated the thrown as he was in love with a divorced Nazi sympathiser which allowed his great-grandad to become King.

It's only after the offence happened that they apologise for it. We should be like the Queens husband, Boris Johnsons' & Donald Trumps' of the world who say outlandishly racist words, just say sorry about it after and continue on with their lives as if nothing happened. The problem for us is that we are a nice race of people. That's why we got into the problem that was slavery. If we had treated Europeans with the same level of suspicion white people treat everyone else, we wouldn't have been so welcoming to them when they ventured to Africa. So, we must be bold but keep the same level of humility we have always had. We must learn to be ourselves once again. That takes time & effort. Self-education, self-acceptance & a self-realisation. We don't need other people's approval to be great. That can only come from within & then is subsequently projected outwards to the world.

Part 2

Interpretation by a Nation

One of the failures of many people of African decent living in the so-called west is that even though the pitfalls of continuous poverty are obvious, some actually participate in its ills. There is knowledge of people like the Krays and many east end criminals that we should abhor. But some young people (A minority) have succumbed to the criminal gangs. In some regards you have to blame many of the adults who chose not to maintain & share righteousness in life.

For many years' hip hop music has been to blame by adults for the influx of youth crime but at the same time they play and enjoy the music. It's fun to listen to yes. The problem arises when that's all the young people hear. People of an older generation had a dearth of uplifting, wise music to counteract the slackness. That happens less in today's music industry due to record sales. There is music of a positive nature out in the public. It's on the adults to play it more when the youngsters are in an ear shot so they can get a variety and not only hear about one aspect of life.

Hip-hop is necessary as it is a way for the underclass to express what they see/hear about in their local area. People are angered by the violence in some songs but forget it is a vicious circle. If poverty didn't go so hand-in-hand with crime, then these people would have to rap about different things. To create awareness sometimes it may seem excessive but for some people life is excessively harsh. The unfortunate thing is 30 years Ago Grandmaster flash released The Message & people still have to go through some of what he depicted in his lyrics. So, rappers are still having to talk about similar things.

When Hip-hop first came about it was a party music. Then it went global with a message but now some are going back to its roots with tracks focused on partying. Which is Okay. It would be great if some of the more popular artist would add some diversity to the lyrics but they tend not to. So, it's the task of the consumer to look for other types of lyrical content. What also would help is better access to uplifting hip hop. It exists, if more people seek out that type of song making it more successful then perhaps, we would hear more positive hip hop stars like Kendrick Lamar. This would help to uplift many of these young people to do more things that are important for society for the social and emotional well-being of the community.

The same goes for movies. I believe they are even more influential than music. Many men & women have become famous for violence. You can't see a gun in a recorded song. The morality of these so-called heroes is usually low also which definitely doesn't help. So, it's a must we counteract the crime and violence in film with films from other genres & cultures. Eastern & African cinema has many films containing wisdom. We also need to infuse a love of reading. Our classic books were all written to enhance the intelligence of Black people. To help bring awareness of another perspective. This opens the mind which is what these young people & older generations are crying out for. Reading also uses mental energy which is a must for all. But all of these mediums are forms of entertainment. Yes, they are influential on the brain, but it's environmental conditioning that is the root cause when interpreting life negatively enough to turn to crime.

Doing things that are criminal is very much so selling out. Doing things that do not give the easy opportunity for the police to arrest you is the best thing as it seems it's a goal of the police to incarcerate as many Black people as possible. This minority don't see that and foolishly make it easy for the police to stop them for no reason and harass them. It's also helps the stereotypers make life awkward for the Black majorities.

All of us need to learn the law. When we are being harassed by them, what makes it easier for them to have their way with us is our ignorance of the law. If you know what type of conduct is correct, this will help to reassure ourselves that we are right when we see we are being wronged. Also, when they make a mistake or lie about the situation you are in, you will be able to put them in their place & subsequently stave of this attempt to bring forth the life of illusionary crime they try put us under.

Another thing that we are confused about is the term to sell out/keeping it real. A lot of people especially the young think the so-called thug life street culture equates to being Black. The way they got it twisted is these are our interpretations of European culture. The baseball cap was invented to play baseball. The hood was made to keep the head warm. The gun was made so Europeans would have an advantage over enemies in war like circumstances. Majority of those people forget that the clothes they wear are all material possessions that are acquired by money. The moment you work hard or do criminal acts for the acquisition of material goods bought from

European or Asian companies you sell-out. We all forget that not investing in the spiritual self or Africa and The Caribbean isn't why we came to these shores. It was all about rebuilding home here & in the place we are from when the first Windrushers came here. Now with the opening up of better communications with Africa we can invest in that continent. But we don't. Instead of investing in the place our heritage is from to make that a place to be marvelled at again or spending our money on African owned business products, we allow our hard-earned cash to be usurped by already wealthy Europeans & Asians.

Even though many rightly feel shame, it's hard to blame Black people who gain an abundance of money and decide to move out of the poor community and not look back. Not to help out the people that they grew up around. That is what the Europeans do when they acquire loads of money. They go to places like Christie's and Sotheby's and spend tens, hundreds of thousands even millions of pounds on art but is that abhorred? When Andy Warhol's painting of Blondie sold for 7.2 million pounds were people disgusted? Of course not. So, when we see that we think why not waste money. Yes, if they gave money to charity or an African village that would go down well but that doesn't happen in this society. We have TV charity appeals that raise about £30-£60 million pounds but at the same time Football teams spend on players, £50 to £100 million pounds. This mentality makes it fine in their culture too hoard & waste money.

So, when we live in this society and acquire wealth, it's going to happen that the things spoken about while amongst the average Black person will be forgotten. Then those Black people who are left still struggling feel aggravated by the said people and then put them in the sell-out bracket. They gain a kind of prison mentality. Like when an inmate has to watch a friend leave prison. It's a bitter sweet feeling having to stay behind & watch them walk to freedom.

Any person of African descent who gets entrapped to this material way of thinking and doesn't delve into the natural African spiritual self is a sell-out. Someone that purposely acquires money over happiness and well-being like most Europeans is a sell-out.

We all have Pineal Glands at the back of a brain but the Africans have the largest. This is said to give us an enhanced sense of rhythm and a better connection with the spiritual elements residing in existence. As it's part of our nature it's a must we develop these aspects continuously. This is Key. We are very spiritual people but while living in this society it's become harder to develop fully with so many external distractions. If it is not acknowledged, the energy within can become negative as society breeds a lot of negativity. When this happens, we see the fall out in the violent temperament in these lost individuals and if it's not violence many succumb to levels of foolishness that is usual amongst the European culture such as Alcoholism or Drug use.

When I travelled to Ghana & Egypt, I noticed that these people were extremely creative. They use the tools at their disposal to develop great pieces of art, showing off excellent craftmanship. This creative essence is instilled in all Melinated people. In the west, similarly we use the tools at our disposal. Indeed, they are different to those in the mother land, even still, we have created many intriguing inventions.

We forget to pay homage to our achievements. We don't revere enough of our achievers. Be proud of the way we have taken European things and have been innovative. Also look at how before we learnt musical instruments there was just folk and opera music. All the other genres have been influenced by the African mind.

The way we interpret European language should be marvelled. Ebonics makes us rhythmical speakers so we have broken up these languages to fit our way of speaking. Literally adding colour to them. Now copied by our fairer skinned counterparts. Many things that we originate has been usurped by Europeans. Like CC TV, The Guitar, The Drum kit, The Fist Bump, Hair Care products, Twerking (Even though to do it properly you need a meaty Gluteus Maximus which most white women can't attain naturally) and as I said, many genres of music like Rock & House have origins in the African mind. What is called Urban culture by some is blatantly Black culture. But when white people start to appropriate our stuff it gets rebranded by them. Whether it be Justin Timberlake, Eminem, Iggy Azalea its Black culture being re- interpreted by white people. When Run Dmc made the Adidas Tracksuit fashionable did they change its name? If we start taking up Morris Dancing would they change its name? Black people dancing around a pole, dressed funny the same way white people do it would be just Black people doing Morris Dancing Aka cultural appropriation. But no matter if the fall out can be considered negative it is a glorious thing to see Black people achieving things in a world that is controlled by people who want to keep them subjugated.

"A Summer of violence comes from a winter of delay"
Martin Luther King Jr

Another aspect of Black society that some people get called a sell-out for is not being so-called Woke. Aware of the oppressive regime and being vocal or visual with your activism. What the accusers don't realize is being a radical Black person is also a response to interpreting this society. If they didn't feel like they are in an oppressive regime they wouldn't have to rebel against the system. They wouldn't chant down Babylon as in a harmonious society where people of African descent were appreciated the way they should be; we'd be more harmonious people. Protesting for equal rights and justice isn't what is normal to anyone. Ya get me? It's a direct response to acts that they feel are wrong. No other reason. If white supremacy wasn't an issue, there would be less to complain about.

Even some white people have a similar complaint. The underprivileged white people that are even called by their own people Poor White Trash. They don't reap the benefits of the so-called White Privilege. They get knocked down, looked down upon, not as far down as a Black people, but they are not made to feel a part of the establishment as well. Due to us being a small percentage of the population, Black people will live amongst the working-class white person. Seeing them struggle & be disgruntled also. You have people like those that live in the north of Britain that are proud of that northern heritage. Like Scousers who outside of Liverpool are sometimes frowned upon by their brothers & sisters from the establishment, but still feel good about that lifestyle. You have some that are not so proud and have elocution lessons to eradicate their accent to give them a better chance of being a part of the privileged. Which works and like the Africans that acquires wealth they move to the level that puts them socially above their more authentic brethren.

As well as Africans a lot of these underappreciated white underclass members have often become radical and fought against this hierarchal system. People forget how radical Guy Fawkes actually was. He who wanted to blow up the houses of parliament, but unlike in the film V for Vendetta he failed and to make a point of his failure every year we celebrate this misguided man by burning effigies of him. But this is another blatant show of what can happen to an individual that goes against government. So, people are fearful and subsequently don't always follow through with their anger at the leadership. But when that fear is ignored, they do make a real impact. Many have made attempts to readdress the balance of power.

Look at the many white women that have made fundamental changes for their rights in this patriarchal system. (Imagine how much harder it would be for Black women if they hadn't) Paving the way for great women like Rosa Parks, Angela Davis, Ella Fitzgerald, Billie Holiday, Maya Angelou, Jane Goodall, Mother Teresa, Whitney Houston, Oprah Winfrey, Frida Kahlo, Kathryn Bigelow, Ava Duvernay, Aretha Franklin, Junko Tabei, Nadia Comaneci, Indira Gandhi, Mariah Carey, Althea Gibson, Billie Gene King, Harper Lee and many others.

Yes, it is true that many tend to sit idly by and allow the status quo to carry on. There are white people that have fight like Julian Assange who are ready to protest with/for similar changes now. It's a must that liberal white people actually do more than just talk about white privilege. Those who actually acknowledge it exists but aren't happy that they are affluent and are able to access it & can see all those who stand and watch them take advantage but can't do the same. So, they fight to make changes in society that would make things a level playing field because they want change also and actually try to bring it forth. Unfortunately, that doesn't happen on a regular basis so the majority of those knowledgeable people with privilege are waste men and women.

Society as a whole needs people from all cultures who know that things are not right. Who can blatantly see that inequality exists and want to make society a better place to live for all. Those who openly admit the wrongs in this so-called civilized democracy and are ready to discuss (And act upon the discussion) ways to move forward to a place where every community has a level of affluence that is acceptable to live in for all. All Communities are invested in correctly. Instead of just a small percentage of people holding all the wealth as it is in our way of life now. Everyone is accepted and is thought of as an asset to society.

Part 3

Racist Rhetoric.

People who are of a racist mentality have not seen the truth about the development of the human species. In the BBC documentary The Human Journey presented by Alice Roberts, it was made clear that ancient Africans migrated across the world. Some ended up in Asia & others in Europe. The ones that ventured to Asia mated with an archaic human species called Denisovans their offspring are said to be the ancestors of people who reside in Asia & the South Pacific. A similar occurrence happened when the ancient African mated with the Neanderthal which gave birth to the European. This explains why Cheddar Man (The oldest human remains in the British Isles. Found in Cheddar Gorge, Somerset) had dark skin. Eventually they contracted Melanin Albino turning their skin translucent. The Neanderthal had shorter upper bodies which is a trait still visible in the DNA of their descendants. So, when they show stories depicting the Neanderthal and say we are all descendants of them, they are either purposely lying to you or are ignorant about this subject which leads to the spectator falling under the same shroud. But a lot of people get shown a false view of existence that they may have issues with. As the people in the west get told things that are predominately meant for Europeans to witness & consume. We don't need sunblock or make up to add colour to our cheeks but you still see Black people using these products as they have lived amongst the advertising campaigns designed not for them.

The crazy thing is that white people don't have any reason to be racist. When you think of the despicable acts, they have done to others they should be the ones that are treated with vilification on immediate view but it's not like that. The ignorant Europeans fail to see their stupidness and treat people badly because they look different.

The problem in calling for stronger punishment for people that perpetrate racist acts is that these people will still be racist. Whether they go to prison or are fired from their job they do not change their view on other races in fact it may just fuel the fire. Obviously, the main problem is racism so that is the issue that needs to be addressed. Europeans need to ask why are we still racist? Why is it still relevant in society over 50 years since Martin Luther King Jr and Malcolm X died? Was Dr King Jr Bullshitting when he told us about his dream? Is brother Malcolm a fool because he spent, gave his life, trying to stop racist rhetoric? In the 1970's James Baldwin asked the question How much time do you want for your progress? Still, we have this despicable problem in the world.

It's not the fault of the ethnic majority. We did not teach racism. Europeans are self-taught racists. We are the victims of these crimes against humanity. Would you ask a rape victim to solve the reasons why they have been raped? White people have this issue that they need to eradicate from their minds. Has there been a psychological study into this problem? Why this problem arises? If not, why hasn't that been done? It's a necessity to finding a solution to this learnt behaviour.

A considered mass defiance of the ignorant people who continue to follow old European colonial ideals is needed to rectify this situation. The education system could help a great deal also. A major problem I see is there are still young racist people. How do we stop young people from acquiring this way of thinking? It's scary to still see people under 20 years old acting this way. It would be understandable if the last racist were aged 50 plus but that isn't the case. Somehow a percentage of young people are also learning to be racist. No baby is born racist. If you look into the eyes of a baby, they do not see prejudice. When kids of different nationalities play together you will notice all they care about is having fun. Race is far from their objectives. It's as they learn more about the world and hear/see viewpoints of their elders that their opinions are formed. Racism isn't hereditary it is learnt behaviour. If when they go to school, they learn true history that counteracts the racist rhetoric they hear then it would be much harder to form that hateful viewpoint. Practically impossible. If Caucasians can educate themselves to send people to outer-space & eliminate small pox, then in theory they should be able to learn to quash racism.

The police need to change training methods. They are training weak minded fearful thugs. All police forces treat the under privileged unfairly (Without fear of the consequences) but the worst culprits are those in North America. Why do they always shoot to kill? They don't show them how to shoot in the arms & legs which makes more sense but maybe more difficult as the target is smaller. Any police officer with a gun should be an expert. Able to shoot a needle. Not these fools they give guns too. And do they teach them to be racist? It seems like it. Really, they should have in their training regime an anti-prejudiced program that they go through to eradicate any prejudice's before they put on the uniform. But that doesn't happen instead they're fearful of us. Probably due to the athletic exploits of men like Mohammed Ali. This I feel has given them a scared view, so when they see a big Black man, they feel they would lose the fight without a gun, without shooting them somewhere. It's always going to be hard for the worlds Black people while this current training is still happening that maintains the ignorance that leads to families dealing with grief.

Perhaps a racism database would help. It would hinder racist acts if people/organizations felt that there is some consequence to their own actions. This database could be checked by anybody. Making it easier to detect if a person has the potential to commit a racist act. It would help companies who don't want that type of individual in their corporation. As well as a way to find the people to help. When these people are found, a neutralisation of their wicked ways should happen. Perhaps a program of racial rehabilitation is needed. This would help vanquish the racism that resides in these weak-minded people.

If a change is going to truly come, it's time for white people to really stand up. For many years now great Black people have stood up & shared amazing words to open up hearts and minds to the plight of Black people. The problem is they fall on too many deaf ears. Racist people will not bother to hear these orators, read the X amount of literature because they are racist. For me it wouldn't make sense for a racist to listen to a Black man due to their hatred. The best way to get through to these people is for their fellow white people to speak to them. Liberal Europeans must now join the fight. Not just for injustice, but to eradicate this blot on the human race. Even if laws are changed to have harsher sentences for perpetrators of race hate crimes that will not curb the enthusiasm for wicked mentalities.

The rest of industry should take note of the No Room for Racism campaign adopted by The Premier League which needs to transcend football and be administered everywhere like Coca Cola. With key figures from the white community being ambassadors for the cause. Indeed, the solidarity that taking a knee brings to the battle is nice. I commend Colin Kaepernick for his career wrecking endeavours & I understand it when a national anthem from a racist country is being performed. I don't agree with these strong people lowering themselves though at other times when we are meant to be taking a stand against racism. The Black Power Salute would be a far stronger image. Emulating the heroics of Tommy Smith & John Carlos from the 1968 Olympics. Another way the World of Sport could help is to have, after the divisive national anthems, a song that promotes unity amongst all like Rhythm Nation by Janet Jackson or The World in Motion by New Order.

The Black Lives Matter campaign is a good start. But the only reason that has credence in this time is because of the insidious racism that is always around. Destabilise the institutional racism & wondering whose life really matters becomes irrelevant. The best way to do that is all who want change to work together to get rid of this unfair burden. Not just walking around and shouting. Not looting & destroying livelihoods. But organised peaceful demonstrations outside the places these powerful people congregate. Consistently day and night until they legislate changes. Not having any sympathy for the interruption of these heathens' lives who dampen the call for change.

Boycotts would be extremely beneficial to changing things as well. People forget how much power the corporate world wields over the government. If a large percentage of people boycotted the major soft & alcoholic drinks, confectionery & fast foods, sports & designer wear companies for say 3-6 months/until they join the battle, those big brand corporations would start to put pressure on the governments as they have a tremendous amount of economic power that the people in power would have to listen to if they spoke up in our name. Mass strikes would also help. If you consider how the Covid crisis diminished the economy of most countries, you can see how the lack of people power hinders the economic growth of a country. The wealthy need workers to exploit to make mass profits. Without a workforce, financial clout crumbles. So, if people used this power to help introduce harmony into our society, demanded that the rulers of the world's dis-ease make the world a better place by relinquishing their lust for the societal ills that prejudices manifest from the world would be more hospitable for every.

Part 4

Give us the Teachings of his Majesty.

The church would be a major contributor to the destruction of this conflict. If it divulges the truth about the ethnicity of the main protagonists of the religion. In the Bible there are many passages that involve people from the Empire of Kush, now known as Ethiopia. In most depictions Kush is spelt with a K being the first letter of the word, but in the Bible it's Cushite with a C. Francis Cress Welsing mentions this first passage in her book The Isis Papers.

1 Miriam and Aaron began to talk against Moses because of his Cushite wife, for he had married a Cushite.
2 "Has the LORD spoken only through Moses?" they asked. "Hasn't he also spoken through us?" And the LORD heard this.
3 (Now Moses was a very humble man, more humble than anyone else on the face of the earth.)
4 At once the LORD said to Moses, Aaron and Miriam, "Come out to the tent of meeting, all three of you." So the three of them went out.
5 Then the LORD came down in a pillar of cloud; he stood at the entrance to the tent and summoned Aaron and Miriam. When the two of them stepped forward,
6 he said, "Listen to my words: "When there is a prophet among you, I, the LORD, reveal myself to them in visions, I speak to them in dreams.
7 But this is not true of my servant Moses; he is faithful in all my house.

8 With him I speak face to face, clearly and not in riddles; he sees the form of the LORD. Why then were you not afraid to speak against my servant Moses?"
9 The anger of the LORD burned against them, and he left them.
10 When the cloud lifted from above the tent, Miriam's skin was leprous —it became as white as snow. Aaron turned toward her and saw that she had a defiling skin disease,
11 and he said to Moses, "Please, my lord, I ask you not to hold against us the sin we have so foolishly committed.
12 Do not let her be like a stillborn infant coming from its mother's womb with its flesh half eaten away."
13 So Moses cried out to the LORD, "Please, God, heal her!"
14 The LORD replied to Moses, "If her father had spit in her face, would she not have been in disgrace for seven days? Confine her outside the camp for seven days; after that she can be brought back."
Numbers 12 extract from the Bible.

This clearly shows they were not white and we're not too happy about being that skin tone. Now the reason they were turned white was because they were upset that Moses only communicated with God and also because Moses's wife Zipporah was a Cushite. The Cushite's were Ethiopian. Meaning Moses's wife was African and his children also were of African descent. They do not in any way throughout this chapter speak about her skin tone or racial differences making me insinuate that they are of the same race as Zipporah. Moses wasn't the only major figure to have an African female companion. When Abram and his wife were struggling to have a child, they asked one of her handmaidens to help fill the void and she eventually had Ishmael. Ishmael's mother's name was Hagar and she was African Egyptian.

"And Sarai Abram's wife took Hagar her maid the Egyptian, after Abram had dwelt ten years in the land of Canaan, and gave her to her husband Abram to be his wife. And he went in unto Hagar, and she conceived: and when she saw that she had conceived, her mistress was despised in her eyes." – Genesis 16:3-4

"And Hagar bare Abram a son: and Abram called his son's name, which Hagar bare, Ishmael. And Abram was fourscore and six years old, when Hagar bare Ishmael to Abram." – Genesis 16:15-16

Another thing that would make impact on the race relations is the knowledge of King Taharka (Spelt Tirhakah in the Bible). This is 1 of the Bible passage that contains his name.

__2 Kings 19:9__ - And when he heard say of Tirhakah king of Ethiopia, Behold, he is come out to fight against thee: he sent messengers again unto Hezekiah, saying,

Now if you delve into the history of Ancient Khem, what most who don't know its true history will call Egypt, you could come across the 25th dynasty. Which I like to call the final Kingdom. This was when Kings and Queens of Ethiopia/Kush took back control of Waset, a place we know as Thebes and ruled the land. King Taharka was the 8th ruler in this dynasty. He lost the power in Khem to the Assyrians. They went back to Sudan/Ethiopia and continued the Kush empire for another 1000 years. So, these people would have been well known and revered in that region.

If you look at the map of East Africa and the Middle East, you will see that they could've had connections between the two lands quite easily.

Map of East Africa & The Middle East

King James Bible
Are ye not as children of the Ethiopians unto me, O children of Israel? saith the LORD. Have not I brought up Israel out of the land of Egypt? and the Philistines from Caphtor, and the Syrians from Kir?

Christian Standard Bible
Israelites, are you not like the Cushite's to me? This is the LORD's declaration. Didn't I bring Israel from the land of Egypt, the Philistines from Caphtor, and the Arameans from Kir?

This passage is one that has major significance for our race and the origins of this religion. It clearly states that they came from Egypt which we know but a lot of people forget it's in Africa (Not the Middle east as the BBC News would have you believe) and a large percentage of the world do not know that the people that ruled and inhabited these lands were dark skinned. Also this passage shows God to be the same worshipped by other tribes including the Kushites.

This truth shows that the Amen probably derives from Amon Ra of Egypt and thus Christianity probably derives from the spiritual teaching of the time. Also, in Kush they worshipped Ptah who is the creator God. The name Egypt comes from The Greek Aegyptus which is their translation of Hwt Ka Ptah which means the House of the Spirit of Ptah. Even the Greek Ptolemaic empire took its name from Ptah and is part of the name of one of the most famous Greek Egyptians Queens Ka Leo PT Ra.

If you read just previously you will see that the Hebrews left Egypt, Africa and moved to the middle east. When you take this into consideration coupled with the knowledge that the Prophet Mohammed was of Arabic decent (Some literature says he was dark skinned also) & the Buddha was an Indian, then you come to the conclusion that none of the major religions were created by a European. Showing that some of the greatest minds that have transcended into people to move them to spiritual excellence came from ethnic origins that in recent years have been ridiculed and vilified by people who are ignorant religious followers/masquerades.

Due to having to learn history from a European point of view our world view has been distorted. If you have a wider understanding, it's apparent that great people have come from every part of the planet. The Most High created us so we could inhabit different parts of this amazing world. We are products of our environment. Every continent has picturesque places that have lit up the souls of many. Which is why, when you delve into some of the magnificent minds of past and present, they all have an equalising quality. Love.

The uncomfortable truth of the matter is when all are exposed to the Anglo-Saxon white supremacist world view, everyone no matter the scale feels lesser about people in the groups that are included in the ethnic majority. To maintain this, facts and key figures of history and biology are withheld from the general public. Once the misguidance is disclosed in some way shape or form it's obvious that supreme excellence has come from empathetic people. Most importantly that we are all equal and we all should learn to treat each other that way.

So, these aspects of this religion should be brought to light in the common arena at least to be discussed. Showing the African heritage in the Bible will definitely make changes to these racist minds especially when a lot of the racists go to church and ignorantly quote the Bible when trying to justify their racist way of thinking. But even with all these excerpts and many other instances of Africans in the Bible there is one question the church should ask everyone that goes through its doors. This question would go a long way to help change the hearts and minds of racist churchgoers. Taking into consideration the most important figure in the Bible. Who had bronze skin & hair like lamb's wool might I add. Was Jesus Christ Racist? The obvious answer is no he Loved all. And when you consider that the region was far more multicultural than we've been led to believe, he could not have been prejudiced in anyway. It was the Roman overlords who had a problem with the people around them. So how is it that members of his congregation are racist now? The leaders of these people need to open up their followers to the truths that are there in plain sight but ignorance holds the masses back from the real ancestry of the Bible.

Taken in a tomb at the Giza Pyramid complex Cairo, Egypt

Part 5

Hidden Histories Shall Set Minds Free.

Taken at Karnak Temple. Luxor, Egypt.

At a young age I learnt the Ancient Kamau (Egyptians) were dark skinned Africans. Instantly I became proud to be of the same race as them and sceptical of the British education systems' implementers and wondered why they lie? This question kept reoccurring over the years during which I had the problem of thinking these thoughts and living in England. The majority of the information I consumed on said subject is content by Europeans for Europeans and this is the root of the lie. When Europeans tell the history of African people it's always distorted. For the last 600 years they have been lying. That's many generations. It could be imprinted on their DNA to hide history about Africans and subsequently believe the falsity.

Khufu, Cheops & The Sphinx. Taken at Giza, Cairo, Egypt.

In June 2019 I ventured to Egypt to confirm for myself   that the European controlled system has been lying to the public about the ethnic origins of the people of ancient Khem. On the walls of the tombs and in the faces of the statues I saw African people. The people on the walls had brown skin and it was obvious to me that the features they depicted in the pieces of art were definitely of African descent. In the 40-degree heat I also realized they were sun worshippers thousands of years before sunblock was invented.

Akhenaton's wives Queen Kiye & Nefertiti worshipping the sun. Taken at the Cairo Museum.

Blanketing of the truth leads the public to be more susceptible to thinking Lower Khem was more prominent due to the Pyramids being there. But if you delve into the truth you will see that the 3 most important Kings were from Upper Khem, King Narmer/Menes, Mentuhotep & Ahmose 1. The three Kings that administered the beginnings of each dynasty were all from Upper Khem. When I travelled from Cairo where the Sphinx protects the Giza Pyramids to Luxor it took 9 hours via coach. A long distance.

This is Mentuhotep taken at the Cairo museum.

Mentuhotep who started the middle kingdom has very dark skin & African features in this statue. Realising that the true power of this ancient civilization came from this part also makes sense of why they started to create tombs in the Valley of the Kings. Like the great Temple of Karnak, Waset (Also known as Thebes, modern day Luxor) was the place where the majority of the art & culture we revere came from.

This is Akhenaton taken at the Cairo museum.

Akhenaton is one of the most famous Kings of Khem, he is said to be the father of monotheistic religion. Plenty has been said about his appearance. But they never mention his thick, full, juicy lips. His broad nostrils. Traits of African people.

This picture also taken at the Cairo museum is The Famous Tut (Pronounced Tehuti)-Ankh-Amon & his wife Ankh-Esen-Amon, Notice the colour of their skin, hair & robes

The Kamau on a boat taken at the Cairo museum.

These were a highly educated people. With knowledge we're still utilising in our modern world. They also knew how to create different coloured paint. So why would these intelligent people depict themselves in the wrong colour. Unless they didn't & these revered people actually look like the way these super smarties envisaged.

Here you have a Kamau market taken in Cairo
Museum.

Also taken at the Cairo Museum here you have
Nubian Archers.

These are Kamau archers taken at Cairo Museum. As you can see the Nubians are darker than the Kamau but both are highly Melanated.

This is Queen Hatshepsut taken at the Cairo Museum. Her facial features are predominantly African like most people from North East Africa.

Here Queen Hapshepsut is on a statue outside her temple in Luxor. You can still see the brown colour on the faces of these statues as the sun hasn't faded that part.

The reason there is so much confusion is due to the Coptic & Greek rule in Khem as we now use the Hellenic & Arabic language when naming the Kamau people & monuments. When they infiltrated this land, they also revered the culture so they learnt it from the native people. They also learnt mathematics that we still use today. Euclid, Pythagoras & other Greek scholars all studied in Alexandria. These & the Roman rule came at the end of the civilization.

In fact, it was the Romans who suspended the pantheon of gods' influence over the people when they introduced Christianity & banned the worship of gods like Ptah, Tehuti (Thoth) & Amon Ra.

The Pyramid Khufu at sunset. Giza, Cairo. Egypt.

The sun sets behind this Pyramid every day.

Another period of history that common people are ignorant about is the division of Africa. A lot would have heard of Shaka Zulu and his empire. His Zulu Nation was said to be larger than Napoleons. Unfortunately, he came up against fearful gun wielding loyal British subjects who did not care if they fired their weapons upon people who were at a disadvantage. (Which they decided to glorify in documentaries & films like Zulu Dawn) Yes, they fought well but it was always a losing battle for them. Quite reminiscent of what goes on in places like New York and Minnesota today. This loss lost those Africans a lot. Not only did European governments vow to dismantle any form of African unity while they have Europeans in that region. But the iron grip that is wielded over the continent allowed the people who immigrated there from Europe to steal land, amass great wealth and terrorise the people via apartheid.

If you read the book the Destruction of the Black Civilization you will see that Europeans used internal division to help them in their slave conquests. One of the tactics they used was to team up with a tribe & fight against their enemy. When they happily won the battle, they would betray the people they were fighting with. They didn't just take slaves from the tribe they just beat. They also attacked their partner in battle and took them as slaves also. There are so many other atrocities that is detailed in this book by Chancellor Williams & others that are a must for people to read/investigate to have a broader view of world history. What makes these evils worse is many companies were formed via these acts, keeping/maintaining the wealth of these European overseers. The wealth made by these slave companies helped to kick start the Industrial Revolution.

A prime example of the bleeding of African people is in Haiti. The reason there is so much poverty in Haiti is because it had to pay the French Government Independence Debt ever since Toussaint Overture left the fight to liberate his people in the hands of misguided men. They liberated themselves in 1804. But in 1825 they had a demand from the French government of 150 million francs to compensate their former slave owners. Eventually they settled on 90 million francs (21 billion in today's money) which was paid in 1893. The had to pay interest on the major payment which has devastated this island for its people. They finally finished paying the interest in 1947. As well as these payments they wanted a 50% discount on Haitian exports. They have yet to be able to bring themselves out of the poverty trap the people of France allowed their government to set in motion.

Another attempt at controlling a people by not allowing them to be unified is happening in what should be called Arabia. The Sykes-Pico agreement was a betrayal. When in the First World War Thomas Edward Laurence (Laurence of Arabia) enlisted the help of the Arabian people. He said his government would help to give the Arabic speaking people their own land. The Sykes-Pico agreement gave the French and British governments the ability to carve up Arabia between the two and create countries like Jordan, Iraq, Syria, Afghanistan and they became subjects of these European empires. As well as this slap in the face there was the Balfour declaration. The Lord Rothschild of that time signed the document that gave the Zionist Jews the piece of land they called Israel. Using terrorist Attacks and war they have expanded on their territory illegally and left Palestinian life a living nightmare.

Another instance where a Lord Rothschild has had impact on another part of the world is when he kick started oppression in South Africa. A lot are rightfully discourteous when treating statues of Cecil B Rhodes but fail to be insolent to the Lord Rothschild of that time as he was the financier of Mr Rhodes. Rothschild sent Rhodes to South Africa and paid for land on which they opened up diamond mines on. The company created was called De Beers & has become one of the biggest diamond merchants in the world. A large percentage of the diamonds used in wedding ceremonies are from this company and mines bought by Rhodes for Lord Rothschild. The wealth he acquired gave him the power to rule in South Africa & initiate apartheid.

In the Americas there used to be civilizations whose monuments we revere. Aztecs, Mayans, Olmecs, Toltecs and others. Now we have heard of these but a lot of mystery clouds how they were wiped out. This is because it's another shameful part of European history. It was Cortez & The Conquistadors that led to the disappearance of these peoples. As well as carrying the military they carried diseases like Small pox to help wipe out over 90% of these people. Cortez and others also burned down villages, raped and pillaged these peoples after using the military against them. It wasn't only Christopher Columbus who set in motion the destruction of these people. I implore you to investigate how Cortez destroyed Montezuma's empire. He was the last real ruler of the Aztecs and his ousting led to the downfall of the empire.

We mustn't forget how ex-British people immigrated to America then terrorised and subjugated the Native Americans. A people from the Americas that have been totally forgotten are the Arawak Indians. They lived in the Islands of the Caribbean. They were also wiped out by the Brits. Like the Spanish they wanted the islands and didn't care how they got them even if they used genocidal techniques.

These acts and many others around the world have left these places destabilised to an extent that many of the inhabitants of these places no longer want to live there. So, they travel far to seek pastures new. When they get to the European shores, do they get welcomed with open arms? Are they helped to settle in easily and develop a life on a par with what they see advertised? (They wouldn't travel to these places if they hadn't seen images of it that made it look attractive) On a par with the indigenous peoples. Hell no.

Don't get me wrong many Europeans have done good things with & on the behalf of other cultures. I mention all of these historical acts to show the horrific things that many populations are still struggling with to this day. They have yet to be put right by the perpetrators of these crimes. So, it's left for its victims to try, with help from Europeans that understand the fight and no longer want to see things that give them racial shame & disappointment.

Part 6

Unity is Strength.

When delving into the identity of Black people and what it means for a person of African descent to claim to be Black, it can get quite awkward, due to the fact there is so much diversity in our community. The Ancestral lineages of each prominent country is immense. You have many nationalities that have different cultural customs and histories. Within that each family has a different background and within that each member of the family has different interests, hobbies, ideals and maybe even beliefs. Also, within our race you see different African countries and Caribbean islands mixing. So, when you ask each individual what it means to be Black? or Where are your family from? Depending on the upbringing of the questioned the answer will be different. Life experience for a Black person that lives in Los Angeles differs from someone that resides in London. If you ask that question to someone from the Caribbean the resulting answer will differ from someone born in Africa. Then you have to add other cultures' influences into the mix, as we, like other people strangely enough, are able to learn about and enjoy other cultures. All of these differences are incarcerated in our collective, which is why when stereotyped by other people's it's very annoying. Yes, we may enjoy Fried Chicken, rice and peas but Fish and Chips is alright as well as a Korma curry & Pizza. Yes, Bob Marley, Fela Kuti, Jimi Hendrix, Tupac, Jennifer Lopez & Mary J Blige get listen to, but many of us have heard and enjoyed Beethoven, Madonna, The Beatles & Frank Sinatra. Our tastes are diverse. There are many mixed-race people whose parentage is of African descent & another culture. Who, even if they grow up not intermingling with other Black people, due to the way the world is not colour blind, they will affiliate with the So-called Black culture. Also include the descendants of Spain and Portugal's part in the slave trade, people we now call Latin American. Brazil has the largest African population outside of Africa. Just listen to the music from this region and you can hear the African spirit in it. Then there are the people that sometimes try to separate themselves by saying they are North African. One of the many tribes of Africa, they have forgotten that there mixing with Europeans has lightened their skin. These Africans forget that when the Moors ruled in Europe, they had dark skin. Like the Egyptian on the front cover of this book many of them are Black. Also, the many indigenous people of the South Pacific. The Aborigine, the Maori and others consider themselves to be Black. As well as being dark skinned they also have felt oppression so understand the fight that many of us have withstood. Many years ago, I saw a documentary called The Coconut Revolution. About the revolt against the environmentally destructive mining going on in Bougainvillea. As well as being very inspiring these people were very dark skinned like a Masai warrior from Kenya.

When you look into this notion of our colour to some degree it doesn't make sense that we are called Black. Not everyone of us is this complexion. There are so many different shades of Black. As I have mentioned there are many facets to people of African descent. If you are called Black but are not that in actual skin tone it can lead to a confusion. A justification of their own skin tone has to be administered. Learning to Love the colour of one's skin is a necessity in a world when young Africans are constantly shown negative images of themselves coupled with so much white excellence displayed. So, phrases such as I'm Black & I'm proud can have a powerful impact on someone who suffers from low self-esteem stemming from a societal inferiority complex. Which can lead to many using Nigga as they still feel like one because they have physical freedom but not mental & monetary emancipation. Some have used it as if sticking 2 fingers up at the established originators of the word to say I'm here and what! (It will always be a shame they haven't come up with another word to use)

A better way to help would be to hear people saying Black is Beautiful, Great, Exceptional. Bask in the glory of your African heritage/Blackness. Encouragement always goes a long way. There is also a self-affirmation that the term Black incorporates for all who are dark skinned & have aspects of African in their DNA. Pertaining to the movement it can give its professor a sense of inner power. The more people feel that in their core the more togetherness we will feel. So, it's understandable that a substantial amount of African people would use this term when having to describe who they are. Don't forget using this term is not just for self-gratification, it also proclaims an opposition to the old colonial white supremacist way of thinking. In a world where some people need to be reminded that we are trying to move forward progressively & will never allow them to go back to that ignorant mentality. Until we all live equally, we only use these terms because we have to, as the human race is divided mentally.

Problems that have arisen are inter island rivalry, discord between indigenous Africans &

Caribbean's & of course Gang Warfare. To combat the divide and conquer formula used on us, Unity is a must. Whether it be via a word like Black, finding an African God to follow or a new philosophical understanding. There needs to be that Dreadlock mentality.

"One Dreadlock is stronger than One strand." Dead Prez

If one of us is interfered with in an unjust way, the consequences are dire for those instigators as they have to face the full race. Oppressive people would think differently if they knew we were united, they would have more to contend with. While disunity prevails, we are susceptible to underappreciation & being openly dishonoured without any consequences.

In the west Black people spend an estimated 3 billion dollars a year on material goods and the entertainment industry. But is this reflected in the advertising and media world? The majority of faces you see in these industries are white. This has become an issue that causes identity problems amongst non-European people that reside in the west.

Within the Europeans there is a blindness. They don't understand what the lack of imagery does. Yes, there are some but not enough. There is hardly any resemblance of people from Asia, South America or the South Pacific and African people struggle also to get themselves into the mix. The fallout leaves a lot of young dark-skinned people having low self-esteem and even worse many are now damaging their hair and skin to fit in with the European style. Many people have started bleaching their skin and so many more are afraid to grow their natural hair long for fear of being ostracized by the hierarchy who employ them. But for the time being white people will continue the Status Quo.

So, it's on us to show positive images of ourselves. There are many and with the advent of the internet we can share them with ourselves. It is on us to show our Black leaders in the many different Arts, Scientific & Academic industries as well as the Sporting Heroes and Musical Geniuses. We must learn about the scientists/doctors etc. to share that knowledge with others. Teach about intellectuals like James Edward Maceo West inventor of the Foil Electret Microphone that is used in most electronic devices like, Hearing aids, mobile phones & laptops. Things that are vital to all aspects of life. If it wasn't for the microphone, we wouldn't be able to appreciate Film, Music or Live performance.

We must start to display images in our homes of our Black achievers and inventors to counteract the lack of diversity in the media world. The Peters projection Map of the world should be placed in every home. Making the unequivocal statement that The Peters projection shows the true proportions of the continents & I do not except fakeness.

There is plenty of inspirational information out in the public to sustain our minds but we must seek it, delve into the history books that actually have been written about the many hidden African figures. For instance, the richest man ever to have lived was Monsu Mensa a King from Mali. He's just one of the amazingly strong stories that can be learned about the continent of Africa & the Diaspora.

Ideally, they would teach these things in the European schools that we attend but they don't. So, we cannot rely on these schooling systems to teach what is necessary. Another thing that should be taught in schools but isn't so we should teach it ourselves also is the science of dark skin aka Melanin. We are all

99.9% the same, so Melanin and the effects it has on the body is vast & needs to be common knowledge.

We all have different degrees of Melanin. The more you have the harder it is to see the flesh underneath the longest organ in our body. Just like when you have a blank piece of paper and mark it with a pen. Yes, Melanin makes the skin darker but it also is in the Hair, Nipples, Eyes, Gums, Internal Organs, Blood & NeuroMelanin is found in everyone's Brains. Anything with natural colour contains Melanin so obviously other animals have it as well as being in fruits and vegetables. At its root is Tyrosine an Amino Acid which are the building blocks of life. So, realizing everyone has Melocytes within them is a must for all ages. Reading books like Nutracide The Nutritional Destruction of the Black Civilisation by Laila Africa will inform the reader on Melanin as well as how eating Melinated foods enhances the metabolism. It would be better for everyone to know the main difference amongst the races is the level of transparency the skin has; everything underneath tends to be the same. About 99.9%.

One of the issues we have internally is not feeling equal which is why we are always calling for it from other people. Forgetting we are all equal in the eyes of The Most High. A lot of us do not feel highly of ourselves to be on a par with others as all they know is, they were descendants of slaves or colonised people. If you delve into the rich history and see The Most High resides in the hearts and minds of these peoples that were inspired to greatness, then a realisation sets in. People of African descent are powerful. We survived the greatest atrocity Europeans have set in motion as well as before that and since then African's have done many glorious things in and outside of the world's biggest continent. Awesomeness is ingrained in our souls and acknowledgement of that is what is needed for all Black people to really rise and take back the equality.

Equalities should be expected and if there are people who try to go against them, then they are the foolish. They are the ones to be ridiculed and so be pariahs of society. In a world where people strive for Peace, Love and Harmony somebody that has this level of ignorance in their mind will be abhorred. All of which comes when we all are seen through the eyes of the highest beholder and see the beauty in all races.

Which brings me to another aspect of moving to a better world. Unlike Europeans we must make a point of learning about the peoples and histories of other members of our human race. Because that would enrich the lives of all and be beneficial to curtailing ignorance amongst ourselves as we live in a world where we learn too much about European heroes and exploits (Usually from their perspective) forgetting that Europe is just a part of the world & the majority of the world's inhabitants live outside of it. Knowledge of the ethnic majorities will also open up a greater dialogue amongst people who have been disconnected. Now in a multi-communication world it would make sense for these people to have more interactions.

All races not just Africans have been made to feel inadequate due to the whims of the white man. It's on them to fall into line with the harmonious minded. It's time to show the way forward. If they want to stay in the racist past so be it. Righteous people will just look at them and laugh very hard, probably shake their head in shame also.

Since people from the Caribbean came to these shores other members of the world have ventured here.

In modern times these people have been called refugees. Like we Caribbean's they seek a better life than what they came from. They were not welcomed with open arms. Used to maintain the menial jobs workforce and they have been shown how prejudiced Europeans can be. Unlike us they haven't been as vocal in expressing their aggravation with aspects of this society that are obviously wrong. We have been speaking out in our own name over the years. Not realizing our remonstrations also help those other nationalities, as they all have had to deal with ignorant attitudes. They start to consider themselves Black as their culture, in their eyes, is bland to them or exclusive and either enjoy aspects of ours or feel appreciation for it and become affiliated with the struggle.

They can get behind our movement to help us and themselves. When we speak, we look like we are just grumbling to some people, but if other races tell their truth and also express how they feel about racism, that would help us all. The fact that other races have had to deal with this prejudice proves it's not just our fault and there is an institutional problem many European people have. As well as it being more obvious to us, it would make good natured Europeans take even more note and see that this epidemic has to be curtailed by mainly themselves with the help of the world's ethnic majorities.

And the expectations from Europeans is unacceptable. Why do they not do the same? When in their culture you are expected to take on the culture & adhere to their ideals. But some of the things may go against the culture you are from. If a Muslim goes out with friends and they will probably go to the pub and that will cause a problem. If the Muslim sticks to his religion and doesn't drink he will have to watch his friends become inebriated while he stays sober. There are other situations similar that can arise where someone from another culture will feel awkward. Now when things are the other way around do Europeans take on board the culture they are visiting? A prime example of this is the Europeans of South Africa. Do they have an accord with the indigenous culture? Do farts smell like flowers? Of course not. For some reason it's hard for Europeans to step out of their comfort zone and get involved in learning a new way of being.

Now another issue we need to rectify is something I mentioned could Unify us. At this current time a lot of us lack spiritual upliftment. It is an issue that plagues many of our young and old. The knowledge of spiritual matters can bring a deep internal strength that is missing from a large percentage of us so we automatically struggle to look up & stay righteous. Some don't have any faith in organised religions as they feel they have not helped Black people rise and be who they should be. A lot of them don't see the value in just being an average citizen who works for an oppressive regime, keeping the Wall Street fat cats rich and the people poor even though they and their ancestors worked 10 times harder. Lack of spiritual knowledge can cause a series of frustrations. Why be in a system that doesn't really care about them. Some are very angry at not feeling welcome in the society, so lashing out seems a route to take.

A problem for them is they are not told about what always drives the people who are oppressed to access the internal knowledge that The Most High is with them. Obviously, it is not common knowledge of what intestinal fortitude it takes to stand up against the power structure that causes harm to righteous people & fighters for freedom. These collectives are strong individuals who don't want the system to care about them as they see the leaders as wicked and choose to oppose their actions as they bear witness to the heathens' acts. If the essence that fuelled people like The Wailers to sing the song Exodus, about a movement of Jah people, was infused into the young hearts and minds then stabbing each other needlessly would-be nonsensical acts for these guys. But their bombardment of these positive vibrations is not continuous and it's not openly discussed among Black people on a regular basis. Only a few walk with a higher spiritual ethos and sometimes feel awkward when addressing these issues to other members of the community. But lack of spirituality is not entirely our fault. This apprehension to speak spiritual truths is the fallout of living in a Spiritually Inept Society.

Part 7

Spiritually Inept Society.

For many years' Black people have been fighting against oppression. But the plight against the so-called Man wasn't really listened to or believed by people of the West. They didn't realise that the people they were being warned about we're holding them in bondage and we're actually repressing them as well. But since September 11th 2001 and the rise of Internet websites like Infowars and Young Turks' TYT.com as well as movements like Q'anon and Black Lives Matter, people have started to be more aware of the hierarchal regimes that controls these political systems. People have become aggravated to know that it's a small percentage of our population who own the majority of the world's wealth. They are now in the know about the bankers and corporations that harvest the material power and do not include the general population in sharing the spoils.

When people express their disdain about this insidious controlling system & how the masses give up their civil liberties too, they tend to get ridiculed, made a mockery of by being called a conspiracy theorist. They are made to look/sound like a crazy ranting miscreant. But those who shout these names are the ones who live in fear of an alternative truth. If they admit that the conspiracy is correct then they would have to change their whole world view & probably have to join the fight against the global elite. They would have to acknowledge that these theories like the others are for people to have a better understanding of a concept or system that is unknown in part. Just like before Gravity, the Big Bang & Quantum Physics (Theories that can't be seen & verified with the naked eye) were discovered these so-called conspiracy theorists come up with conclusions to questions they have about the way the world is run. If these rulers were more open, less clandestine with their actions/dealings/interactions with each other, then people wouldn't have to speculate & come up with conclusions that are more than likely very close to the truth but perhaps a bit inaccurate in some parts.

Unfortunately, not enough people are Woke. The general population live and get caught up in their own individual lives & don't actually know/acknowledge that certain networks/institutions exist, such as the Spy network. These undercover trades' people think only happen in the movies like James Bond are real. Like when politicians act debauched, people are left in a state of bewilderment when seeing these things manifest in the news. Ignorance of the way the world works has become the reaction to these industries amongst the spectators.

What needs to happen is full disclosure on who really runs the world, How & why they have acquired this much power via their daily dealings & what's their purpose? Then the rest of the world will be able to see if they have our best intentions at heart or if they're just a bunch of selfish bastards & if they're really keeping the worlds wealth to themselves then how do we exterminate their power & re distribute it amongst the common people?

The modern world we live in is unfortunately a social construct spawned by materially minded men. This thing they call society has been developed over the last 2000 years or so but had a considerable acceleration due to the advent of the Industrial Revolution. Society has come from the belief that a democratic way of leading the people makes sense to all parties. Which leads to the people being dictated to by one leader. The people being orchestrated into what we call the state or country or city. Whether this constructed project is beneficial to the population of created cities or not is irrelevant due to their subservience to the hierarchy.

The populace willingly give up civil liberties as they have to become believers in the state, worshippers of the political arena. Due to the electoral process people are led to believe they have some power in shaping the way their country is run. Adhering to what the leadership ordains regardless if they want it or feel that it's the correct decision. The powerful elite have the ability to administer the police and military which makes it impossible for the general population to collectively oppose the government through fear of the repercussions. They give the politicians the ability to shape society, laws and policies that have been implemented throughout the years of power and control. This is so they can prey on people's poverty/need to make money. This need, to work for these capitalists keeps people constantly in the wheel they wield. This lack of complete freedom has left members of this society seeking release from the pressure put on them via state manipulation.

Indoctrination into the capitalistic mentality gives people the craving for non-structured activities such as pub drinking, watching content that distracts us from reality, shopping for unnecessary unwanted products or drug taking. Stemming from the insecurities that manifest from not being able to capitalise as well as others this semi-deprived mentality can lead to a depressive thought process that breeds acts of an unscrupulous carnal nature & brings down the collective society. This negates the possibility of our modern world being considered a civilization. We do not live in a world of civilised people. Some are but the majority live for foolishness. Are humans prone to this corrupted way of being?

When we look at older civilizations, the one thing they all had was a deep spiritual belief. The Aztecs, The Mayans, Ancient Khem, The Greeks, even The Romans and the Moors all had what we call belief. To them it was more like a knowing. They still did some abhorrent things but to their saving grace they thought spiritually higher so weren't as wicked and didn't have as many inventions that can cause destruction to the planet at their disposal. In our scientific world we have created many things that astound us but at the same time shame us. We learn to fly planes then attach guns & bombs to them and use them on our fellow human. We create the Internet but it includes child and animal porn. Just a few examples from many of how we belittle our own achievements & stop ourselves from being civilised.

A lot of things that make mankind mourn itself are schools of thought that we would annihilate, probably wouldn't even come into fruition if we were more spiritually inclined. This would warrant craving for experiences that bring people together in serenity. Creating events that bring inner and outer joy instead of only the external constantly being stimulated. People wouldn't need depraved activities to be free as true freedom comes from a sense of internal balance developed via spiritual learning. Enhancement of the human experience ends in Spiritual Enlightenment not with greater muscle definition, medically induced hallucinations or getting somewhere faster via an earth damaging 4 door gas guzzler. We live in a world where people become internationally renowned, shout the person's name like in a Beyoncé concert because men & women get murdered by a police force.

The industrialized mentality is a cancer. We super predators have had a devastating impact on habitats containing vast arrays of species in a quest for land development. We lack a Symbiosis with nature. We do not associate ourselves with our fellow mammals & plant life. As we think we are superior. We fail in our actual role on this planet. We should have a more humanitarian way of thinking. Everyone not just certain people given that particular title. That is part of our genetic makeup we do not acknowledge as it comes with a lot of responsibilities. If we ate more foods, used more products that enhance our well-being, we wouldn't need to utilise so much plastic packaging & clear so much land. We'd grow more foods ourselves. We would harness eco-friendlier power supplies and relinquish the destructive constructions as our whole way of thinking is to promote planet well-being.

You wouldn't see continuous news reports of war containing devastating weapons and we would curb the death toll regardless of the conflict. The conflicts probably wouldn't arise as you would assume the leadership of our countries would actually contain wise people unlike now. If conflicts did come about it would diminish quicker than it does nowadays as wisdom would prevail, giving the leaders the foresight to see how to come up with a resolution rather than prolong the battle and continue to allow warriors to murder each other. These leaders would try to stick to the commandment Thou Shalt Not Kill. In fact, these wouldn't just be words quoted every now and then to prove a point to a young delinquent. They would be sayings to use to deliver a rounded thoughtful, peaceful, human being. But unfortunately, the major religions of the world are all failing to administer a harmonious civilization hence our Spiritually Inept Society.

One of the key problems in our western world is the lack of repeated positive words/songs on a daily basis. Yes, Muslim society has its issues that could be changed/redeveloped but one thing that they could share with the West is the regular audible prayer broadcasted to the whole country every three/four hours. A constant reminder of what we are working towards. This would curb the enthusiasm for evil acts after hours. If when getting inebriated a prayer/uplifting saying or song gets heard by the soon to be reprobate's, it may shift the thought processes into being respectful of our species. Some may scoff at the request for some sobriety but why do you want to allow temptation, instead of redemption? Think of all the people, young and old, family and friends of those who suffer from alcohol induced racism, violence, rape or murder. People victimised by apathetic attitudes mixed with a so-called spirit called Vodka or Brandy. Why do we give these sick inducers such an inspirational name? Trying to excuse dis-ease that makes us feel better about needing to be inebriated.

Social alcoholism is another issue that should be addressed. It must be an issue if many people cannot go out and socialize without alcohol. We are hiding in the West a serious collective alcoholism. Why do we feel we have to use alcohol to lower our inhabitations to feel comfortable amongst our fellow human? There seems to be something a bit wrong. Yes, alcohol can be enjoyable to consume but do we need it that much. There's a good reason why most healthy athletes choose not to drink alcohol excessively. Think of it like this, if you are having a coffee with a friend and they slur their speech and act aloof. Then when it's time to get up and go they stumble and struggle to walk, so you have to hold them up, while walking gingerly they start to vomit repeatedly, at that point you would probably phone an ambulance. But if you are out partying reactions like that are fine as alcohol has probably been consumed.

I must also mention how our over consuming of alcohol impacts the environment. Every Monday and Thursday Pubs, Clubs, Restaurants, Supermarkets, Shops and Off Licenses get deliveries of Wines, Champaign's, Ciders, Beers, Vodkas, Rums, Ports, Sherry's, Brandy's, Tequila's, etc and soft drinks/chasers. They are transported from across the world so you can enjoy forgetting about the pollutants these methods of transportation release into the atmosphere. I don't need to mention what happens to many unfortunate people when some drunken idiots get into vehicles. Is our reliance on Alcohol and other self-harming external pleasures a good thing? Does that make us a developed society? Yes. A good one? This is the real question.

Part 8

Why's Society Sick when Religion is Rife?

Christianity is failing the masses when you consider the way things have been panning out over the last few decades. The modern western mentality drives a craving for things that are of a carnal nature due to the consistent bombardment of the predisposed brain by the capitalistic corporate media who have no regard for the well-being of the consumer when advertising products that cause harm mentally and physically, all for material gain. Ignorant consumption of said imagery has created a callous thought process that is enjoyed by the majority of people in the West. This is causing the planet to deteriorate ecologically but even though there are consistent warnings they do not out way the outpouring of content that tries to get people to use the products/materials that cause harm. Everyday a multitude of car adverts are on television. Even though we know they're exhaust fumes are not helpful to the environment and they are one of the world's biggest killers.

When you consider what we do with our money, all the so-called goods we purchase that are destroying the planet. How do you think a Jesus Christ figure would react if he or she actually set foot on the current shores of the US or Europe to witness what we are doing? The late great was supposed to have died for our sins but a lot of people don't give a fuck as they want to continue the sinful behaviour. Say for instance Moses came back holding the stone tablets that contain the 10 commandments in his hands. How many people would be shamed into making a change? He'd be upset to see how many people would fight their intuition to live more righteously. If he parted The Red Sea again, he'd struggled to get everyone to take heed as a lot of them would have seen Magneto levitate a stadium, how can he compete with that? All joking aside they would have to fight hard to convince the stupefied sheeple to make a change from the material to the spiritual.

Now there are plenty of worshippers around the world that follow the word of Christ. Inside and outside of the west. So, how's the church lost its influence over the others? Partly it's due to it being over 2000 years old and stuck in its old ways. A lot of the ideals set out were for a people of a different age/mind-set. None of them flew on a plane, used a mobile phone or watched TV. These factors make it hard to compete. Our backward world-view has led people to see a hypocrisy from the church. Many parts of our modern way of life contradicts the lifestyle administered via church doctrine. Many wife coveters & adulterers like Prince Charles would find difficulty with these statements & for a soldier in Iraq or a NYPD officer its exceedingly hard to uphold the commandment Thou Shalt Not Kill.

Also, what makes it harder for people are crimes perpetrated by members of the Catholic & Christian faith in Jesus' name such as paedophile priests and pastors. Having to hold up a Bible in a court of law that people see as corrupt and unjust. The religious wars. Naming the first slave ship Jesus. Taking in money to create material wealth amongst its hierarchy even though Jesus abhorred money. The list goes on.

It is not easy acquiring faith and maintaining it when it's not conducive to the modern career driven person who does their job so they can satisfy their want for uselessness. Leaving the soul unsatisfied. An undiagnosed depression. That has many doing strange and unusual things to get a form of gratification, like S&M. So how can the Christian world regain a foothold amongst all the chaos? Well take a look at the other religions that come from other parts of the world and have spread to the West. As opposed to having a doctrine that stays stuck, they need more fluidity, move with the times. Instead of promoting the judgmental side they need to promote the more Self-Aware, Self-Love and subsequently internal Universal Love. All of the great Sages that have spurned the different religions sort out after & acquired Enlightenment/internal Peace. Jesus said the Kingdom of heaven lies within.

"The kingdom of God does not come with your careful observation, nor will people say, 'Here it is,' or 'There it is,' because the kingdom of God is within you"
Luke 17:20–21

He stood humbly on the mount and preached his words against the anti-spiritual system in power. An advocate for Peace and Love so much so his words were anarchistic to the Roman elite. That activism is what is needed from the people who should be his successors. Fighting for the spiritual freedom of the people even if you create conflict with the state. They need the same form of revolutionary suicide set by the father of their religion. Until they take an inspirational leadership role in society, we will struggle to have a civil society.

It would be extremely beneficial if a spiritual group created a political party and joined the political arena. We cannot leave it up to the current rulers as they distance themselves from having any spiritual influence and refrain from speaking in an uplifting way that would inspire people to do better. They are not allowed to, as not to be divisive or seen as religious. Even if one of them wanted to they would probably relinquish that ethos as soon as enough realisation sets in that they don't have any real power to speak freely and have to fall in line with the corporate world. They & the Bankers maintain the power in modern society and have a need to promote the material minded manifesto rather than anything close to spiritual doctrines unless it can make money or be used to promote something that makes money. They disparage true peace and harmony as it rarely makes enough money to satisfy the multi-billionaires.

Why is the elite in control when people should have more power? Why do they give up so much of their liberty to the rulers of the world?

If everyone was of an uplifted mentality would we really change? What would that do to the elite?

Part 9

The Cultural Revolution.

When people acquire a sense of Enlightenment, they tend not to venture to things that are unnatural to find joy.

A problem that the common people have when being ruled by an elite like ours is their willingness to keep the wealth to themselves. The fact people automatically know what type of individual is being represented when you speak about the global elite shows that there is a separation. There are a so-called high-class people who do their best not to associate with the middle and working class. These selfish people do not welcome the people they look down upon. Thinking they are uncivilised but recently I heard an interesting stance on the word civilised. Connecting the word with welcome saying that a civilised set of people are overtly welcoming. Maybe even to their own detriment like Africans that welcomed the European that subsequently enslaved the continent and colonised it. Most average people live with Peace and Love in their hearts so are welcoming until they are wronged then things change. When did the common people wrong our leaders for them to be so stand offish? A people who do not share, do not welcome and keep themselves in their own community but expect to be worshipped.

What makes this situation worse is the masses are fine with it. Or if they are not, they don't do enough to change the situation. Most people don't mind the hierarchy lording it up in our faces. In fact, it makes them want to be more like the hierarchy, these people that disrespect them all the time. A prime example of this is when the Grenfell tower in London's Royal borough of Kensington & Chelsea burned down. Members from the richer part of society visited the now homeless people and not one of them offered them a bed for the night. This would have been a moment when someone like the Queen, who came and allowed the survivors to shake her hand, could have taken up the opportunity to do something Giving, Helpful, Beautiful. Did she offer to take even one or two people to her lovely home, her large Palace, full of empty rooms? She could have offered a wondrous gift. No way would that happen, she prefers to watch people from her closed gate so they had no chance of that invite. And no one expected her and her fellow members of the hierarchy to do something like that. The reason for this is they have spread their separatist mentality to the rest of society. They have led everyone to believe the main goal in life is the acquisition of wealth, to be like them, to be a single-minded driven individual.

When said people turn into a human vulture, they justify it to themselves. When they see the bank balance. Other observers may see them as an abhorrent prick but understand how much of their soul they have sacrificed so they excuse the person, maybe even feel sorry for them. Some are envious of them also and wonder how they have pulled off an apathetic outlook. People put more effort into their career instead of their family. Spend more time at work than with loved ones. Unfortunately, most are duped into this pursuit of wealth instead of pursuing happiness. This makes people that, even though they may come together to drink with friends and family, have an underlying rivalry which keeps us separate. How can I make more money quicker than you? If the answer involves hurting a fellow drinker, they may have no qualms in doing so and willingly do something to get one over them, maybe even enough to cause pain. You even see this type of thing happening in families between so-called loved ones. It just makes it easier to apologise after if you have a strong relationship but the cut will be deeper.

This separation has stopped the people coming together in sweet harmony. Giving this ruling elite enough division to rule, there isn't enough unity to make real change right now. It's hard to do rallies/protests to make better choices about our society/environment when some people drive, some people get public transport, some people work longer hours than others, some people buy/eat food/drink in plastic containers some don't. Some dispose of them properly, some don't. Some fight for racial harmony, some are blatantly racist. For various reasons people are not on the same page and the book is large.

How often do you watch a wild life programme and they mention the dwindling numbers of these wondrous species Lions, Tigers, Elephants, Hippopotami, Rhinos and so many more, even insects & plant life are in a serious struggle for survival at the moment due to our wayward consuming. But do people shed a tear for the destruction of the environment? We live in a world where more people care about their favourite sports team than the welfare of Bees or Gorillas. People, grown men cry when their team loses a Cup final. The camera team always pinpoints the people seriously upset over human beings running about losing and still getting paid for it. Have you ever seen one of these losers go up to a crying family and console them, give them a hug? The closest I've seen to that is Eric Cantona's infamous Kung Fu kick into the stands when a racist spectator vocally abused this Frenchman and he chose to retaliate.

Part of the problem is we all care about our own individual toys more than things that can be enjoyed communally. We gather together for some things but usually for our own singular joy. Attend events that we can dress up and feel good for, but getting to an event that isn't for personal satisfaction such as a protest or for the promotion of harmony, we fail to attend unless we're in lockdown and there's nothing else to do. It's odd to think the environment comes second to a pop concert. To sing you need air. We need the trees to breathe. Our created pollutants in the air can be cleansed by the trees but we watch people drive, waste electricity, waste gas. We waste a lot and create waste that we don't recycle. We dump or burn it causing more harm to the environment but love buying more things that can cause harm. Over and over again forgetting it's the things we do that create the world we live. So, the more we do things that creates harm, the harm will be done. Ya get me? To me it seems simple but a vast majority have yet to really grasp that concept. If we start to strive for goodness, then good things will manifest. We should work at doing things that help the planet, consume only products that do good for the environment, make pacts to recycle and leave the rainforest alone, finally. How much paper do we really need especially in this technological time we live in?

In our current world there is a long list of things we do that has a devastating effect on our ecosystem, wildlife and our fellow human beings that happen to be less fortunate than others. The acts of wickedness and foolishness are common knowledge. There is enough literature and media content that people should be aware of the terrible ills happening on a daily basis. Unfortunately, these apathetic news watchers sit idly by watching horrific moments on a TV screen or read all about it in a newspaper & do nothing to change it. Hopefully there will be an insightful future generation that live with an ecology that has been healed. If they do, they will look back at people of our time as mentally ill. We have a kind of Kamikaze ideal. We can go on doing damage to ourselves. Let's keep using things that kill the planet. Yeah, they are fun, they make me feel good. A mad Crazy world mentality.

Even though the second world war ended and treaties were agreed and signed the world has been at war ever since. The conflicts haven't been on the same scale but news broadcaster have consistently been telling us about the warmongers that start and continue these battles that do not hinder global warming. In fact, they have enhanced it. There's a lot of heat dispensed by weaponry that is released into the atmosphere. As long as I've been alive there has been some governing bodies that disagrees with each other so much they war. To me it doesn't matter which side that is agreeable. War is wrong. Destruction to be despised. These leaders love war though. So, it has to be grinned and bared by people who hate war. When most countries have a huge war budget, like the members of Apollo 13 we have a problem. When the US have spent money on building over a thousand nuclear bombs, like the members of Apollo 13 we have a big problem. Especially when they are the only country callous enough to drop an Atom Bomb on another people and they did that after dropping fire bombs on the Japanese people who lived in wooden houses. It's a major worry when these countries have so much military might. These countries that are led by volatile leaders that don't care about the civilian victims of war when sending troops to help to maintain conflict. It scares me. I don't expect them to bring peace to us. Even during the Covid Crisis where people are on lockdown and the economy is struggling, they keep that war budget nice and healthy. These people/Corporations that make military weapons & vehicles must love the atrocious mentality of these leaders. I wouldn't be flabbergasted to find out they manipulate countries into building battle grounds. They thrive from that pain regardless of whose side they are on.

I heard the US are starting to send its army to Asia. Opening military bases in that region. They may be expecting to rage war on China, hopefully not. These politicians think like the Emperor in Star Wars, that you can have these wars to create peace. Foolish people. It's foolishness that makes them think the only way to administer that, is to destroy the enemy. I thought listening and compromising leads to acceptance & Harmony?

Part 10

How did the world come to be like this?

There are actual diagnosed mental health issues that are constantly being spoken about. The people who commit suicide. Alone and feeling inadequate enough to take their own life. How did the world come to be like this? The rise of obesity. People who no longer care about their health and well-being enough to overpower their lust for food. How did the world come to be like this? Even though there is an abundance of wealth in the world every country has elements of poverty. People struggling to find food & water even in affluent countries like England. How did the world come to be like this? Hard drugs usage is still ongoing and they keep on inventing new ones because like with obesity, people have become so lost in their depressive state of mind they fail when trying to overpower their lust for drugs. How did the world come to be like this?

On the news you see the world at war. Over the last 100 years there has been some conflict in almost every part of the world. The major battles that took place in Europe, Iraq, Afghanistan, Vietnam etc, between so-called soldiers and then the ones in the streets between so-called thugs. All because one side or individual wants something the other has, they feel the need for but it's unnecessary as they survived without it before and we are an intelligent race that can come up with ingenious ways to live. But caring goes out the window when the lust that sends people to war overpowers what is right. How did the world come to be like this? Every country around the world has a war budget that if they stopped these conflicts and used that money for humanitarian/environmental changes that are really needed society would benefit. It saddens me to know that wouldn't happen. I would love to have at least 1 whole year where there isn't some form of military campaign going on in the world. How did the world come to be like this?

People spend a considerable amount of time, either going to establishments that contain so-called specialists in changing their original appearance or trying their own hand at making themselves look good. Some even inject toxic chemicals such as Botox (Botulinum Toxin causes the disease Botulism) into their forehead or seek a doctor to infuse engineered materials into their frame to create a physical image they feel is more acceptable to others. Making billionaires of men and women who prey on the insecurities of others. How did the world come to be like this?

People of African descent have faced oppression via Europeans but other people have felt the same administered pain. For instance, in India the tactics used by the British made Mahatma Gandhi starve himself. Whether learnt inadvertently or not, these tactics employed by Europe have infiltrated to other systems & have been repeated by countries causing conflict in Nigeria, Ethiopia, Egypt, Zimbabwe, & D.R.Congo where they battle for the control of Coltan (Used in the production of mobile phones). In far too many places like Brazil, Palestine, Libya, Lebanon, Myanmar, China/Hong Kong, Korea, Turkey, Belarus & Australia where the Aborigine is restricted by repressive European immigrants. How did the world come to be like this?

The multiple conflicts that have caused people to flee their home, becoming a refugee. Then when their horrific journey ends and they seek somewhere to set up home. So, they can feel some solace. Do they get welcomed with open arms by the government & it's people? Do Black people relish the cold? No. They get tolerated. Those that don't want them in their vicinity make their disdain obvious making life even more uncomfortable for these distant travellers. How did the world come to be like this?

For various reasons people mainly women sell their sexual organs because they know there are many willing clients who have belittled sex to a point, they devalue the feelings they know exist, choose to ignore them as they are too weak to fight the carnal craving. The internal shame, the caring for the woman's mental state and well-being cannot come to the fore as they will interfere with the act of diminishing the soul which to these foolish people is more important. This has led to an industry that encompasses rape, drugs, kidnapping, mental breakdowns and murder. But do these ills stop the main clientele maintaining the infrastructure of this sickness in society? The morality of these people keeps prostitution thriving. Continuously finding new ways to get around its apparent illegality. How did the world come to be like this?

Sadly, we see many people that live in the street. It's normal to walk past someone in a sleeping bag or a cardboard box begging for money. When in the midst of homeless people, the affluent tend to look at them with contempt. Forgetting these humans have had a dismantled life journey that led them to living on the streets. Most rich governments no longer build affordable housing. They allow luxury flats for the wealthy to be built though. Many stately homes & warehouse's stand abandoned, while many a homeless person would love to live in some old empty dusty building. If any of them use some initiative and inhabit these empty spaces they get called a Squatter, get marked as a criminal and maybe arrested & thrown in jail. I suppose prison is a roof over their head. We forget this world has so much wealth, millions are spent by NASA to send probes into space & a small amount of people have hoarded the majority of the world's money but do not share it with the needy because like the tramp disdainers, they feel there is something wrong with helping the less fortunate. How did the world come to be like this?

During the So-called Christmas festival people forget to be galvanised by Jesus Christ. So, people waste so much paper on greeting cards, wrapping paper and packaging for presents & food products. The wastage for each household is too much for the environment to maintain, but people won't even contemplate that while worshipping a man dressed in a red suit that promises material goods like the devil. Santa has the same letters as Satan, just the n is in a different place. He probably wears the hat to hide the horns while duping people into causing damage to our eco-system. How did so much ignorance come to be in this world?

Thankfully these politicians don't commit murder as they would get away with it easily. One thing about these people is they make many mistakes. Do things that disappoint and upset voters but yet still due to the way they control the system they get to carry on failing. This form of dictatorship has led us into an insipid predicament. Whether the Covid-19 virus was created in a lab by scientific researchers or the military or it's a mutation caused by the use of pesticides, this is because of what is allowed by the law makers. Who pretend to care but they showed what they care about when their main concern was the economic effect the pandemic had.

When are we going to get leaders that actually make positive changes that help all members of society? That is the type of people who we should be voting for. Members of the public who have a more environmentally friendly, humanitarian philosophy that they utilize to govern. Pre Covid & current leaders developed a society with a lot of ills contained within. Kidnapping young women & turning them into prostitutes hooked on drugs, the police unjustly killing Black people, Spies being assassinated, poverty in every country of the planet, oil spills, the constant wars making refugees of children, part of families that have to travel miles to find a home without conflict. The inhumane treatment of animals and pets, the way co2 levels are at an all-time high due to the mass production of petrol cars, (Unleaded petrol is still petrol and causes far more harm than good) How many newer cars do we need on the road? Consumption of many unnecessary products can be cut to a level that helps the environment but these ills will just continue when we get back to pre Covid-19 so-called normality.

I don't want to go back to normal. To me it makes sense to try for better than that. Do we want to see more protest against the people who hold on to that privilege even though they have murmurs of change? It still hasn't come. Now is the time, while we have the opportunity to administer a new harmonious world. Since 2012 we've been at a cusp. We could continue with the dis-eased world. Watch it become a dystopian place where extinction events happen. Or help it to heal so we can thrive and maybe even build a utopia on earth finally. It's been spoken about throughout the years. John Lennon sung about it, Imagined it. To me it's a shame he could only Imagine. I wish that would come true but I am part of the few it seems. Many would consider that idealistic. Most are not bothered enough to try and bring that type of world into existence. Wouldn't a world full of Peace, Love and Harmony be beneficial for all?

It's hard to rely on the current leadership to bring forth a prosperous civilization. It's their fault we are in this current crisis. Due to decisions, they have made, society is at a kind of half-mast. If a restaurant gets a Cockroach infestation and has to be condemned, does the Environmental Health Officer go to the patrons eating the food, or the waiting staff, not even the kitchen staff are bothered? It's the owner/management that takes the shame. If you or someone you know used to own a restaurant that has a mass food poisoning & if the opportunity to manage another one came up, that rubbish manager wouldn't get that job due to the proprietor being worried about the hygiene of the place.

When I watch the current crop of leadership, I'm filled with disdainful emotions because society's sickness is their fault and I don't have any faith in them anymore. They led us into a state of human ruin. Thankfully I believe in the people. Like before when major upheaval has happened in history, the human race has overcome. This is our opportunity to set things straight. We can create a place where we have intelligent righteous thinking leaders that want to provide a harmonious planet for its residents. Shall we strive for a place where antisocial behaviour is common place or instead have a place where people are appreciative of one another constantly. Is that so hard for us to bring to fruition?

The crazy thing is that the answer is so simple. Easy to administer to the masses and would be something everyone would savour and promote with ease. The main thing that can conquer this soulless death driven mind state that many buy into.

Part 11

God is Love.

We are a nation with no geographic boundaries
Bound together through our beliefs
We are like- minded individuals
Sharing a common vision
Pushing toward a world rid of color-lines

People of the world today
Are we looking for a better way of life?
We are a part of the rhythm nation
People of the world unite strength in numbers
We can get it right one time
We are a part of the rhythm nation

Janet Jackson

Love is the answer. With it more prevalent in our daily lives, life would be improved. If people had a Love of wildlife and our planet that would be beneficial. It would infuse people to be more considerate of the planet. As important as that is, Love for our fellow human being would have a major significance. Love would bring the races & the classes together. Even if there is a deluxe dislike of the content of the person's character, a basic Love of the human condition and what it encompasses can destroy that & the main problems in our society. War, crime, prejudice, prostitution, hard drugs use, the separatist mentality and the willingness to hurt others for their own material gain. All of which would diminish if there was a basic understanding that Love conquers all. We are all equal in the eyes of God, The Most High Loves us all. It is so simple it doesn't make sense that it isn't the main concern for All people.

Striving for goodness, Love, Peace and Harmony gets drilled out of us during school and college. We become hardened individuals; hell bent on making as much money as possible before we kick that so-called bucket. Then later in life a list is created to do all the things we felt we wanted to do that would give us more appreciation of the life we have. Trying not to waste the time left.

Bring back the mentality had when children. Request for wonderful experiences. Seeking people, things that tend to be of a natural basis. They have so much joy and Love to give. Full of hugs and kisses. To them all that is in their mind-set is enjoyment but eventually for them they grow to adulthood and then that childlike quality diminishes even though it is missed and every opportunity to feel that way again is taken up. I'm not saying we mustn't grow up become more mature. But we must develop a society that seeks internal fulfilment that leads to inner Love similar to that inner joy of children.

Even at work. If the management are more inclined to think in a loving way then it will filter out into the workplace, creating an environment people look forward to going like when kids can't wait to get to school. Most adults don't have that want to go to work as they generally are not places that promote well-being, so they spend a lot of time at work thinking about the places and things they could be doing to feel good. Times are changing. We are seeing more spiritual practises coming into the workplace but the main opposition to this will always be the people in power.

One of the things the Covid crisis brought to the fore was something that I genuinely don't mind keeping when normality resumes. The appreciation for the so-called Frontline workers. We who revere the rich now should put these people, who were looked down on, in the highest esteem. I and many always thought they were important especially knowing many of them. Now society is starting to see them in the same esteem which is fantastic and long may it continue.

Obviously, the spiritual ineptness is what the hierarchy want in society as they wouldn't be dumbing down the public continuously. There was a time when people in the West had more communal thinking. This was before the Industrial Revolution when people had to rely on each other more and also after most wars there has been a brief moment of communal peace & togetherness. Now the rulers bombard us with their smokescreen. They simply lead people to believe the world is okay and there is not much we can do to change it other than blindly vote for a new leader. Behind the scenes there is a lot of disgusting and uncomfortable truths. The destruction & plundering being done to the planet and its people so that these wicked individuals can acquire funds to have private islands and do all kinds of depraved acts with money usurped from the people's pockets. It would be extremely beneficial to all if we found out what they really do, maybe horrifying too.

To detract us from manifesting the upheaval needed there is a cascade of distractions. The many obstacles that our brain has to withstand has become too many to handle for most. It is a good thing to keep the mind occupied but, unfortunately, we are not a society where mindfulness is common. Due to the many things that distract us from our internal truths. An intense career, partying hard, supporting a sports team, getting the hair done up, acquiring nice clothes, celebrities etc. People forget to learn about themselves. To know the self. This can cause mental disturbances when weak minded people find themselves alone with more time on their hands and struggle to comprehend who they are truly. Some think of outrageous things to do/feel something satisfying. But it's usually external like plastic surgery, not realising the soul is straining for peace & harmony via self-acceptance.

More and more people are bypassing the quest for foolishness and seeking the within. Which is why you see things like Yoga being popular. But for others the lack of collective social well-being is a problem as they don't have the time or more importantly the know-how to invoke Enlightenment. The only thing we must do now is start to develop a spiritual understanding of life in all aspects of society. From the political arena to the nursery playground.

We humans have obvious differences between us and the rest of the animal kingdom that we belong to. One of which is our ability to choose how we want to live. Spirituality always starts with a question that starts you on a particular path. Do I acknowledge God or do I ignore? If a person chooses to walk a righteous path, they will lead to either find a religion to follow or have a more experiential worship that is less structured and more varied. Throughout time many Sage like people have been compelled to share their internal revelations with as many people as possible.

This has led to many spiritual doctrines that people can learn from.

STEPPING INTO MYSTERIOUS PLACES & SPACES

For the longest of times here I've been standing
At my strongest fighting
The ineptness of western people
I've had moments where energy has been wilting
Exasperated by the weak
I seek happy people with spiritual abilities
Like a Blackbyrd flying high
Making what mankind finds impossible
Soft & easy
Instead, the majority behave like daffy duck after he's
had his beak blown to bits
Absolutely embarrassing.

Graciously guide your gifts from the ground floor
Love has come around
So, take a stance
Enhance your mental majesty
Prime yourself for the penthouse
Characterise chance
A figment of fiction
Reap the rewards of realising
All experiences are dedicated to you
Due to divine law

Please step up to this platform
The simple request of a bored few
Who want you to transform

Quickly like Bumble Bee.
But bredrin unfortunately
This is no cartoon remade into a Hollywood movie
In this reality we wait with the anticipation
Of a diver on the highest board.
Take a stance
Do it fluid
Breath
Quiet the unfinished business
Close your eyes and look within
See the kingdom of heaven
Beautiful Balance, tremendous tranquillity, cool
calmness
Acquaintance with equilibrium
Feel the mysterious vibrations
Shift the polarization
To positive Merkaba via mental transmutation.
Be at one, free the way
Breathe deeply

So now I JC Kamau send out a call
To those who when it's time to move on up
They stall, they cower
Collectively they scramble under an umbrella
When they are showered with true knowledge
The earth's greatest power.

My mind stepped into mysterious places & spaces
It was my destiny to find
The Way Orchestrating Very Divine Awakening
Words.
I translated them especially for you.
So that love can come around.

For me it didn't make sense to read just one point of view. I chose to read the spiritual classics of other cultures. I was first schooled in the Christian faith but that didn't stick as I became mystified when I saw a picture of Jesus for the first time. My instincts at a very young age, around 5 years old I was, were correct as I instantly knew what I was being told about his ethnicity was a lie. Even though I still went to church because of my young age I felt this type of worship wasn't for me. Eventually I became aware of the concept of My Body is My Temple. Then I started to feel it unimportant to go to church & listen to someone preach words what I should already know. That's for people who struggle with sin. I felt wise enough to begin to feel in my own way about The Most High. Not being dictated too. How to Live in My Temple given to me by The Most High is Always between Myself & The Divine Spirit. As opposed to interpreting a book and only reading a book over and over again. Overtime I chose to read and learnt of other schools of spiritual thought. Growing up in an area where Muslims live, I became aware of that religion as well as Malcolm X and the Nation of Islam. I also became privy to the Rastafarian faith via Marcus Garvey, Haile Selassie, Reggae music & informative friends.

Overtime I read The Tao Te Ching by Lao Tzu, The Teachings of Buddha by Bukkyo Dendo Kyokai and George Tanabe, The Gnostic scriptures by Bentley Layton, Plato's Republic, Eco Philosophy. Designing New Tactics for Living by Henrik Skolimowski, The Tao of Pooh by Benjamin Hoff, The Upanishads, The Metu Neter volume 2 Anuk Auser by Ra Un Nefer Amen, Spiritual Growth - Being your higher self by Sanaya Roman, Cry of an Eagle (Ancient Toltec teaching) by Theun Mares, How the world is made. The story of creation according to Sacred Geometry by John Michell, Journey into the

Super mind by Richard Lawrence, S.Q Spiritual Intelligence The Ultimate Intelligence by Danah Zohar & Ian Marshall, Man and his Symbols by Carl. G. Jung, The Kybalian by Three Initiates, The Hermetica - The writings attributed to Hermes Trimegustus edited & Translated by Walter Scott, Shamballa Path of the Warrior by Chogyam Trungpa, some of the teaching of Osun deities from the Yuroba tribe and I also took short courses to learn aspect of the Kabbalah & Advanta Vedanta meditation.

As well as reading a vast array of words on the subject I have listened to uplifting music that have informed me to have a better understanding of something I love. These products of art permeate positivity, but the messages have not had enough of a profound effect on all of us. Songs like Here I Come By Dennis Brown, Elevate the Mind By Linda Williams, Sowing the Seeds of Love by Tears for Fears, Easier to Love by Sister Sledge, Happy by Pharrell Williams, One Love, One Drop, Exodus Album & many others by Bob Marley & The Wailers, Let's Get Free or Die Tryin' Album by Dead Prez, Tennessee by Arrested Development, Didn't Cha Know by Erykah Badu, Woodstock By Joni Mitchell, The Crown By Gary Byrd & The G.B Experience, The What's Going On Album by Marvin Gaye, I Am by Wyclef Jean, Hungry but won't give in by Sade, Forgive Them Father By Lauryn Hill, We Are The World By U.S.A For Africa, The One & Only by Chesney Hawks, Golden by Jill Scott, Can You feel It By The Jacksons, My life by Mary J Blige, All Matter by Robert Glasper featuring B'ilal, Nirvana Album by Herbie Mann, I Can by Nas, Gold by Spandau Ballet & many other great pieces of music are put out to the public to actually change the world. Uplift the masses. Like Bruce Lee who was a force for positive change, expressed insight\inspiration & human excellence to help change people's views on Oriental people.

Thankfully these wise words & visuals have come into my earshot & optical view. Witnessing & hearing this variety about a similar subject gave me the realisation that they are all speaking about The Same subject, The Same feeling, The Same essence, that inspired them to share. They all felt the power within. An energy that gives life and death. From the moment we are born its part of destiny that we die. It's inevitable. The goal is to learn to Love Life. Give thanks every day. Harness & understand the Supreme Incorporeal.

The way of Balance starts from a single point that doesn't exist in our physical realm. It creates a line of spirituality let's say, that has Polarizing Forces, Positive and Negative. Most people fluctuate between the opposing forces. A large percentage of people in the West prey on the negative energies which is why we now have so much hate and apathy on our planet. Thankfully there are positive people who are doing great things to counteract the negative.

Then there are those Balanced individuals who see All and decided to share. Balance comes from meditation, clearing the Mind/Body/Soul and being in a space where you don't feel separate from The Most High. Oneness is acquired, with the energy that has many names. You internally become acquainted with Akasha, Chi, Prana, Ohm, The Force, Ankh Energy, The Holy Spirit. Which leads you to have a better understanding of the self as well as having a deeper understanding of the cosmos.

Once the awakening is achieved a reverence for all life happens. You are more aware of natural forces that we see and are not seen by the naked eye like the Chakras. Most people don't even realise that when they are expressing to someone how they feel they will often point to the middle of the chest. Thinking that they are pointing to their heart. Indeed, they are, just not the physical one. If there was more knowledge of the Chakras, then people would know that the heart

Chakra is situated in the middle of the chest and when it gets filled with emotional energy, we feel it. Which is why we point to it. When you go to the doctor and they listen to your heart you will notice they put the Stethoscope to the left just below the chest, because that's where the heart actually is.

Energy is something to feel as well as touch. An example of what I mean about the importance of energy that most don't understand is Heat and Cold. When there is an abundance of energy, heat arises, the sun is a good example this. Or if a person goes for a run they will heat up and maybe start to sweat. On the flip side of that when energy has dissipated, then things become cold and a human who lacks energy can become tired, slow, maybe even sick.

Energy is all around us. When we see light that is energy. The essence of everything vibrates and the differences we see and experience are energies vibrating at varying rates, vibrating a certain way. Sound is proof of the energy around us. We can't see it. All we see is someone put their lips to a trumpet and blow, move their hand up & down rapidly over a guitar, or just open & close their mouth. Have you ever tried to see if there is a band in a CD? More fool you. Try holding a Mp3. But we all hear, feel & enjoy the invisible effects of sound amplification. We are constantly surrounded by unseen radio waves. Try finding them without a radio transmitter.

In the scientific world you see these so-called intelligent people talking about Dark Matter and Dark Energy. This is the unseen energy that resides in all aspects of life that fluctuates and vibrates to create this existence we have. In CERN, Switzerland they built the Hadron Collider with which they found the Higgs Boson. The so-called God particle. This is said to be in all elements that make life as we know it. We living beings are made up of an abundance of Atoms that contain this God particle. There is a spirit that connects everything and nothing in this and all universes. Spirituality comes from feeling this force from within and working on maintaining an acquaintance with it, he or she. It doesn't matter about what the name you know it by. These are assumptions/guesses, thing's mankind clings too to be familiar with it. Before mankind was even an apparition in The Most High's mind, even before sound existed, The Most High existed. Do we know its name then? We will have to go back into the annals of the Akashic records. Long before we humans could speak and find out what it was then. At the moment of the Big Bang there was no name. Words didn't exist in the form they do now and if we were to lose the power of speech The Most High would still be there for us to acknowledge.

There is a lot of different doctrines, ways of thinking. I like to think Freely. Not being held in bondage by other opinions. Yes, take from other inspirations, but you are the experiencer and you are the living being. Be. Live, Love and Harmonise. Like with Zen Buddhism there isn't a book to adhere to. Learning via meditation and listening to the divine energy that is all around us is their doctrine. Like with the first to be at one with The Most High, who had no name to call, no others to show he or she the way, they felt It, experienced It and loved It from Within.

The quest for true spirituality is completely experiential. Once you acquire that knowledge, be Sage like and Share, Share, Share. Many have, there is so much content. The Dalai Lama has fantastic YouTube videos as well as many others that have developed enough sacred knowledge to be able to eloquently share it with other members of the human population. What we need is to have it so much in the common tongue the hierarchy cannot ignore it.

Hopefully getting them to change because the only other way is for them to be truly overthrown with violent conflict. Which we do not want or need. Part of the problem is that in the past revolutions have been violent, which breeds a society that is born out of conflict, creating a vicious cycle of a continuous Love/hate relationship with the people in power and the ones that want to revolve the way society has panned out.

A Peaceful Revolution should in theory breed a Peaceful Civilization. That type of change to a more Harmonious Loving people would be wondrous. If the majority are more spiritually minded, then we would be more appreciative of one another even if an argument arises. All parties understand that this is a differing of opinion and we could move on even if it leads to mutual dislike, you can move on as we both know the ultimate goal is seeking Enlightenment, Peace Love and Harmony and both are striving for the same thing, so there is always an underlying mutual respect. At one point Malcolm X and Martin Luther King disagreed on how to go about getting freedom for their people but they had the same outcome in mind and were said to want to come together in Unity. Unfortunately, they were both assassinated before that could happen.

But we are all here now and we can come together in Unity. There was a sense of civility between them that we all need. So that we can always move forward in Unison. Under the umbrella of Love, we can Unite. So instead of feeling stranded and alone we can feel oneness/togetherness. Then and only then we will be a nation of civilised people. One nation under the groove so to speak. Nothing will stop us now except us. I hope you can help in the Cultural

Revolution as I like to call it. When all people feel comfortable in their own culture/skin and feel free to come together to direct energy in an optimistic way.

When you consider everything has an opposite so does the planet, it has North and South poles. If you delve into the Electromagnetism of the planet you will understand the negative energies, we emit can influence the planet. Humans are conductors/transmitters of energy. We have the power to take this negative state we are residing in a flip it on its head. But we never have had enough minds thinking in spiritual terms in the Western Hemisphere before. Only a limited few have really had that true understanding. We see it, understand and revere people of that ilk. But they usually are fictional characters like Gandalf, Yoda etc. Not acknowledging that there are many real humans from the past and present who have tried to spread that truth to the mass of people but have failed as their opposition are strong at maintaining their own negative momentum. We have to weaken it with our acquisition of higher vibrational knowledge. Then as a mass we would have the strength to bring to fruition what most of us want. We who want to have that sense of wisdom that the Sages have. They found that light within because it's always in all of us. Like the smile of a joyous child, we are born with it. We just need to seek and find. So, we implement heaven on earth. As we are meant to. As Above So Below. No average human has ever been there and come back & verified its existence so like all my predecessor I'm just speculating. But do you think The Most High's realm contains as much debauchery as on our planet nowadays. It's more than likely an extremely serene space. The type of place we should be administering to our globe.

When that acknowledgement is admitted all that needs to be done is to nurture it like anything else. We are human beings with the ability to learn whatever we put our minds to. How do you think a man like George Bush Jr became President? If he can do that & if George Weah, a footballer can learn to become President of Liberia, we can all learn to be spiritual beings living a true human experience? We can be people whose goals also include seeking internal Enlightenment. It starts with you. Share it with your fellow human. Love them enough to help them make those positive changes. I hope you will and decide to do that ASAP/ now. I believe in you because like you I want to live in a real civilization or a civilised nation that understands and administers the concept behind the great Muhammad Ali quote Me. We.

The Cultural Revolution

The world is a mess.
The vicious vibrations that are internal antenna ingest,
Damages the brain waves.
Sons and daughter's dissatisfied due to lack of divinity
in the commonplace.

Making it ambiguous and awkward to feel blessed.

Finding your inner worth,

In a time of evil on earth is a true test. Separated by

secular scriptures.

Pleasures of a carnal nature are ignorantly expected.

What lies beneath is no longer respected.

Difficult to break away from the ferocious foolishness

Desecration of our greatest temples is a major

violation.

Mankind must manipulate its most magnificent

monuments into marvellous manifestation

Get back to our miraculous psychic sensations

Crystal characters directing energy for glorious

harmonious illumination.

The revolution was not televised because it did not happen.

It's time for us to make that change.

This selfies age we must rearrange.

Peace and unity is the solution.

People get ready for the Cultural Revolution.

A BEGINNING. STAY GOOD. BE BLESSED.

TO BE OR NOT
TO BE BLACK?
BY
JC KAMAU

JC KAMAU
PRODUCTIONS

LET
CREATIVITY
BE
YOUR
GUIDE

Printed in Great Britain
by Amazon